Andrew Grumbridge quit work early to co-found Deserter, for which he writes and broadcasts. He makes music and is co-owner of the Shirker's Rest pub. He'd also be quite happy to do none of this and sit in the park with a tinnie, but you can't have everything, for some reason. He lives in Herne Hill, south London.

Some achieve laziness and some have laziness thrust upon them, but Vincent Raison was simply born with it: a natural, you might say. Did he waste his gift on just skipping school and bouts of unemployment? Of course he did. That is, until he met Andrew Grumbridge at a 'Sit-In for a Five-Day Weekend', where they decided to share their wisdom for the good of humanity. The alternative lifestyle website Deserter was born.

SHIRK, REST AND PLAY
The Ultimate Slacker's Bible

Andrew Grumbridge
and
Vincent Raison

unbound

First published in 2022

Unbound
Level 1, Devonshire House, One Mayfair Place, London W1J 8AJ
www.unbound.com

Text design by Ellipsis, Glasgow

A CIP record for this book is available from the British Library

ISBN 978-1-80018-146-5 (paperback)
ISBN 978-1-80018-147-2 (ebook)

Printed in Great Britain by Clays Ltd, Elcograf S.p.A.

1 3 5 7 9 8 6 4 2

Dedicated to our children,
Billie Mae, Chloe, Ella, Kit, etc.

SUPER PATRONS

CONTENTS

PREFACE

Congratulations! You have bought this book because you want to turn your life around, and that is an important first step. Or perhaps you were given it, in which case you're back to square one before you've even started. Sorry about that.

Have you forgotten how to relax? How to enjoy yourself? Do you run around in ever decreasing circles mistaking dizziness for happiness? Your troubles are over, for you hold in your hand the means to take control of your destiny, to step away from the stresses of modernity, to turn your back on obligation and conformity, or at least hide from them in the toilets for a bit.

What happened to the old you? Happy and carefree, kind to children and animals. The dreamer, the hobbyist, the enthusiast, the collaborator. Impulsive and fun to be with. And what happened to the people you knew who were like that, too? They are all around, waiting, like you, for the call to arms, to duck out of the system and reclaim their lives.

We call them – us – Deserters.

And this is for us (them).

A. Grumbridge & V. Raison

INTRODUCTION

In 2011, the Australian Bronnie Ware published a book called *The Top Five Regrets of the Dying* based on her time spent as a palliative care nurse. Impending death, it seemed, brought with it a clarity of thought, and Ware was surprised how often the same themes came up.

Those five regrets were:

- I wish I'd had the courage to live a life true to myself, not the life others expected of me.
- I wish I hadn't worked so hard.
- I wish I'd had the courage to express my feelings.
- I wish I had stayed in touch with my friends.
- I wish that I had let myself be happier.

For us, the realisation that these feelings were so common-place came as such a shock that we immediately decided to do something about it, ten years later. Was there an anti-dote to such poisonous end-of-life reflections? Perhaps we could ensure, by recourse to the advice of experts (or similar), that such regrets are minimised or avoided altogether. We could share what we have learned. We could create a handbook for a long, enjoyable and regret-free life, lived on your own terms. Although we would have to actually write it; there was no way around that.

This is that book. Later we shall return to those regrets, armed – hopefully – with a perspective that allows us to consider and deal with them more effectively. But for now let us examine the general characteristics of another type. The type that has freed him or herself from the yokes of regret and disappointment: the Deserter.

What is a Deserter?

The Deserter is not one of the herd; the Deserter is different from the crowd; you might even say wilfully abstruse, contrary. Deserters are leaders, not followers. Unless they are told to be leaders, at which point their only desire is to follow. They don't take no for an answer. Nor, indeed, yes. Often they are unable to recall the question.

Independent in thought and deed, you can spot a Deserter sitting on the lawn with their shoes *and* socks off next to the notice that reads 'Keep off the Grass'. Confronted by a sign saying 'Turn Left', the Deserter will be overwhelmed by the urge to immediately turn right, or possibly turn back, or at the very least stand stock-still and spark up a fat one.

Deserters are free. They are the ones who, while you are squeezing onto a train to work, are on the other platform boarding an empty train marked 'Brighton' or 'Kempton Park Races Special' or indeed any train that is *going the other way*.

From what are they Deserting? you may ask. Work, perhaps, or the rat race in general; society, maybe, and certainly *that which they are expected to do*. They are not lazy *per se* but it can sometimes be difficult to discern what exactly it is that they actually do. The Deserter will often struggle to answer questions about work or career at parties or other social gatherings, but that is because they are the wrong questions. Ask not of a Deserter 'What do you do?', ask instead what they *do not* do, and you will receive an answer so fulsome you may decide to get another drink even though you haven't quite finished the one you are holding.

In fact, they often excel at what they do, however little it may be, but find it emotionally and physically exhausting. And so another trait of the Deserter is to take the opportunity for sleep whenever it arises, even if they're not terribly tired: in a car, perhaps, at work, or a funeral.

In short, you might characterise the Deserter as a rule breaker. Not the big rules, not 'Thou shalt not kill', but certainly the rule that states you must work diligently for fifty years, accept meagre wages and be unhappy.

We arrived at the Deserter life through a combination of personal experience and the enlightened guidance of others, many of whom we shall encounter over the course of this book. People like the Dulwich Raider, nap expert and Lord of the Bargain, who vividly recalls his first day at work and his reaction to it: 'I really do not fancy doing too much of that.' He has dedicated his life to that noble goal. He, in turn, was influenced by his 'Mad' Uncle Cyril, who once invited him over to his flat in Clapham for lunch.

'He was nearly seventy and his fridge was filled solely with champagne and tennis balls,' he recalls, breathlessly. 'I knew immediately I was in the presence of greatness.'

Then there's Spider, who was fortunate enough to buy a house some years ago and, when house prices rose, remortgaged it for ever-increasing amounts, netting cash lump sums in lieu of a salary. 'My house is shitting money!' he would cry to anyone who would listen –

mostly the person behind the bar. For years people laughed at him; now he laughs at them while they take notes.

Or there's Roxy, who met fellow slacker Dirty South when she was his boss at one of the UK's lesser-known magazine publishers. Dirty had asked to see her to discuss his hours.

'You know how I currently do three days a week?' he said. Here we go, she thought, another poor hopeful stranded in the foothills of a coveted media career, looking for a leg-up to the summit. 'Well,' he continued, 'I've checked my bank balance and I'd like to go down to two days a week.' Roxy was instantly fascinated by Dirty South's contrarian mindset. She had met the laziest man in the world. They've been friends ever since.

Ivan Osman, on the other hand, is busy from the moment he wakes, feverishly gaming the corporate system in order to hasten the day when he can give shareholders the finger, pull on a pair of Speedos and build the beach bar of his dreams. He works on the inside. We call him the Corporate Deserter.

And then there's Half-life, the Deserter par excellence. Six foot four inches of imminent menace and recalcitrant nonconformity, mostly to be found propping up bars, pinching pork scratchings and getting the party started. This life is funded by alarming poetry, the dole and the on-demand redistribution of herbal wares. Half-life may well, as Osman once remarked, have lived his life 'as a warning to others', but he has also had the most sheer fun of anyone we know, moseying through existence on a desire path towards, if not happiness, then certainly pleasure.

Which brings us to the fundamental characteristic of the Deserter: the proactive seeking of pleasure. They have had enough of deferral and denial, enough of discipline and the toeing of the line, enough salad and sparkling water. *For crying out loud,* they seem to be saying, *pass the sausages.*

'All good things must come to an end,' goes the popular miserabilist saying. Who says so? OK, turns out it was Chaucer, but what he actually said is: 'There is an end to everything, to good things as well,' which is more a statement of the obvious than a maxim with which to wreck your life. So go on, have another good thing.

There may be those who disapprove of our philosophy, on our insistence on wresting back our fleeting lives from the strictures of pointless work and endless production, on our call for freedom and benefits for all. Perhaps you're out of work but hanker nevertheless for a new car or some £500 trainers. Perhaps you're fully employed and an evangelist for some kind of misguided work ethic. If so, this book may not be for you. The coin you tossed landed on a different side and we wish you the best of luck. In the heads or tails of life, may fortune not forget the tossers.

Everyone needs enough to live on, but what we actually need can be substantially less than that which we have been led to believe. The relentless pursuit of money is simply too expensive for the true Deserter, who is happiest with soft furnishings, a book and a vessel of some description; or devising games in the park with a frisbee and a Wellington boot; or strolling aimlessly by the river with a cheroot; or sitting on a train to the coast; selling junk on eBay; writing poems; curling up with a film; strumming a guitar; sketching lilies; beans on toast . . . We could go on, and there are possibly those among you who would say that we are.

In summation, then, all of life's travails present us with the opportunity to slack off, walk away or celebrate little victories. But we need strategies, determination and nerve to become the shirking-class hero that's inside us all, yawning to be set free.

CHILDHOOD

'Growing old is mandatory, growing up is optional.'
– Chili Davis, baseball player

♦ Birth ♦ Early Years ♦ School Daze
♦ Teenage Mutants ♦ High Education

We come into this world not an entirely blank slate. We have certain predispositions: some inherited, some unique to us. We are not, however, born with an inclination for form filling, housework or business attire. Such things are foisted upon us by a society that has forgotten how to have fun, that has mislaid the meaning of existence: to mess about. One minute we're eating crayons or digging up worms without a care in the world, the next we're setting alarm clocks, comparing insurance premiums and calculating square footage. It not only sounds wrong, it *is* wrong.

How does it happen? *Why* does it happen? We blame a society with its focus not on happiness, but on such mundanities as productivity, career and material acquisition, all presented, ironically, as the means to happiness. *Do you mind?* we need to be ready to assert, when we feel under pressure to conform, *I am trying to look for some worms here.*

As a reminder to cling to as much of it as possible, let's consider what happens to us in childhood and hear about the early days of some of our esteemed influencers.

Birth

None of us ask to be born. Our first act is usually a cry of protest at having been forced to do so. We were quite happy where we were, thank you very much. In the warm, in the dark, nutrients on tap. There's no one to tell you to tidy your womb and for giggles you can always give the old placenta a kick. But out we come, into the cold and the light, and if we don't wail at that, we get a smack on our tiny, newly exposed rear.

'Speak for yourself,' said Half-life. 'I gave the doctor a right-hander straight away. Didn't like the look of him.' Pre-emptive action has been a hallmark of the big man ever since.

Early Years

Early childhood is a bit like being rolling drunk: everyone remembers what you did except you. We may remember little, but we take on board an incredible amount of vital information, including how to get around, how to communicate and which parent is the softest touch for biscuits. We eat, we sleep and – if we're lucky – get doted on by spellbound parents.

It is truly a golden era for slackers. We have no responsibility and we also get to be as demanding and annoying as we want. It's no coincidence that when we are at our most helpless, we are also at our most adorable. No one in their right mind would deliver the level of care babies and toddlers need – not to mention put up with *Teletubbies* – without a profound love to see them through.

In addition, little ones are able to take great pleasure in small or everyday things: pebbles, leaves, dead birds, etc. And it is to this childlike state we should aspire when, for instance, we find a discarded armchair overlooking the A205. Should we tut and bemoan the fact that the correct procedures for outsized waste disposal have been ignored? Or should our eyes light up at the prospect of a good sit-down by a busy road? The choice is ours.

Aside from imitating parents and siblings, children learn through play, a method we tend to lose sight of by the time we're perfecting our CVs. By all means give up the dummy, nappies and teddy bears, but don't give up curiosity, playfulness or poking your brother with a stick. How else will you learn? How else will *he* learn?

'Play is the work of childhood,' said the eminent psychologist Jean Piaget. It is our contention that it should be the work of adulthood, too. As the great American cartoonist Berkeley Breathed put it, 'It's never too late to have a happy childhood.'

School Daze

Our approach to school is vital to our future. What we learn there can stand us in good stead throughout our lives: how to skive, mess with authority and unwrap sweets in our pocket. It is also where you make friends, have epic laughs, play games, discover kissing and share music, dreams and possibly half a cigarette before PE. And so we find ourselves at odds with the conventional view that school is where the fun stops and the hard work begins; where you lay the foundations for the life of graft that's to come. It can be so much more than that, despite the homework.

Child labour is rightly abhorred throughout the world, yet even in advanced countries like the UK it's perfectly acceptable for children to return from a day at school to face hours of additional work. All this so that they can elbow their way ahead of other children in life's race to the top. The fundamental misunderstanding here is that life is a race. Life isn't a race. It's a stroll. There is no gold medal at the finish line. It's all about what you see on the way.

Dirty South took a contrary approach to doing home-work, which some would consider extreme. He refused to do it, foreshadowing his future literary hero, *Bartleby, the Scrivener*, whose mantra was 'I would prefer not to.' He figured that an hour of detention every Friday (double or treble if there were additional infractions) was a better bit of business than ten hours of homework spread throughout the week. And even maths boffins might be tempted to agree that ten hours is longer than one.

The Dulwich Raider's tactic for homework avoidance was to attack it at the source. As the bell for the end of the lesson approached, he and his cohort would suddenly become tremendously engaged with the subject and pepper the teacher with challenging questions, leaving no time for them to dictate reading lists and demand essays.

Shirking should start early, even if it's not on the curriculum. Bright students should always be on the lookout for golden opportunities to slip away unnoticed, as truancy is a precursor for knocking off work early. Unfortunately frequent absence attracts attention, so some attendance is unavoidable. But that doesn't mean you are obliged to participate. What's wrong with staring out of the window and letting your mind wander, across the fields and the mountains and the seas, to live with mermaids, or dance with Tall Tracey from the sixth form? Reverie comes easily to the child, especially during double science. Should education be designed solely to rid us of it? To snap us into cold reality? To turn us from dreamers to producers? From child to machine? We say, simply: should it, balls.

In considering reveries, we're reminded of John Stuart Mill's happy pigs: 'It is better to be a human being than a pig satisfied; better to be Socrates dissatisfied than a fool satisfied,' he wittered.

In defence of happy pigs, and indeed fools, they probably spend no more time staring into space than the average philosopher (and quite possibly solve as many of life's riddles) but, crucially, they are happy. Happiness is not a thing to be looked down on, or ignored in favour of the so-called richness of human experience, as Mill saw it. It *is* the richness of human experience, or a very large part of it.

'You are not here to enjoy yourselves!' Roxy remembers

being told by Miss Podmore when she and a friend were sent out of English lit for getting the giggles about Romeo 'saucing' a goose.

'Not supposed to enjoy ourselves? First I'd heard of it,' she recalls. 'Ruined it for me, to be honest.'

Of course, too much skiving can leave the student exposed when it comes to assessment of their abilities, which might affect their chances of getting into a good university; perhaps one with an outstanding reputation for turning a blind eye to loafing. This is why we campaign long and hard for exams to take precedence over teacher-marked coursework. There are many two-word horror stories in the English language ('drum solo', 'last orders', etc.) but 'continuous assessment' is up there with the worst, implying as it does the requirement of a consistent level of attainment and an uncomfortable degree of monitoring. Whereas with an exam, you can cram for it the night before, or simply cheat – a great skill to learn, especially if you're hoping for a career in accounting or politics.

Teenage Mutants

It's tempting to suggest that teenagers could teach us a thing or two about shirking. After all, they are capable of sleeping through earthquakes should they occur before noon. However, their apparent laziness is entirely natural. During adolescence, the release of the sleep hormone melatonin is delayed by a few hours, prompting later sleeping and waking. What is not natural is parents forgetting they were once teenagers and giving them grief for sleeping in. It's not teenagers who have a problem with mornings, it's parents.

Teenagers are at a crucial and often misunderstood stage in human development. Yes, there are the emotional outbursts during which they may accuse the parent to whom they literally owe their life of ruining that life by insisting on the completion of some trivial chore. But that is only because that parent is ruining their life by insisting on the completion of some trivial chore.

They have weighty matters to consider. This could be almost anything from 'Is everything we know about human existence a lie?' to 'Does Alex fancy me?' Or, 'Do bats think it's freaky that humans sleep *lying down*?' The fact is they have begun to think differently. And it's people who think differently that spark leaps in human progress, not the ones who conform. Their oddities should be celebrated, not maligned, though fifteen coffee cups in one bedroom is fucking ridiculous.

One thing that we can learn from teenagers – and benefit from in our own lives – is self-belief. Teenagers' confidence in their own abilities gets them a long way.

How can you not be carefree when, despite doing very little, you know you are brilliant? Surely someone will come along and discover your genius. Even if you haven't written anything but notes. Well, not actual notes, but you do have occasional note-like thoughts, the specifics of which escape you at present.

But before you know it, so-called 'reality' barges into the playroom, kicks over the edibles tray and – like the reverie that was stifled in the child – the wide-eyed insistence that anything is possible, that the world can be a wonderful place, is suppressed by responsibility and obligation. Let no one say teenagers have it easy – the grumpy, ungrateful dirtbags.

Some parents are more understanding of the trials of adolescence than others. Tolerant and sympathetic, they support their child's path in life, wherever it may lead, through triumph and disaster. This is a terrible mistake. If your children find they actually quite like you, you may never get rid of them, which is probably why universities were invented.

High Education

Despite what Half-life says about the Cycling Proficiency Test, it is generally accepted that A-levels are the toughest examinations you are likely to have to face. If you want to pass them, that is. If you don't, they're a cinch. Your reward for the former, should you choose to accept it? University. Three glorious years of cocking about in a new town, going to parties, making new friends and learning about something you might even be interested in, for once.

Ah, student-dom. Finishing school for idiots. Salad days. The best years of your life. And all for free! Oh, no, sorry, it's fifty grand. Should this put you off? Not a bit of it. Yes, the loans are hefty but hardly anyone will ever pay them off before they're wiped from the ledger, and you only have to pay it back in dribs and drabs when you're earning over a set amount, like a tax. Take the money and run, we say. Or, as Osman suggests, take the money and buy crypto. Either way, it's better than work.

In fact, Osman got a 2:2 in business management from Liverpool University and came out richer than when he went in. 'I repackaged my entire curriculum on the fly and resold it online to students in the Far East for $999 a pop,' he remembers fondly. 'I went to my finals in a stretch limo.'

Half-life took a rather different approach, coincidentally at the same establishment. He arrived on day one of a new academic year not to commence studies, for he wasn't enrolled, but with a huge bag of weed to sell to grateful students. Business was good and he was on campus so often that eventually he signed up to show prospective new students around. Latterly, he would even drop into lectures and was never shy of telling the lecturers where they were going wrong. 'I might even have ended up with a degree,' he recalls, 'if I hadn't had to go to prison, like.'

Meanwhile, the Raider enjoyed his time as a philosophy student so much – either grappling with life's meaning or watching *Scooby-Doo* until the uni bar opened, which turned out to be the same thing – that, two years after leaving, he went back to do a postgrad degree. 'I tried work but it really didn't agree with me,' he tells us. 'They say getting a degree prepares you for the world of work but in my case it just got me hooked on cheap booze, two for one deals and lying around in my pants. Or somebody else's. Happy days.'

Which reminds us: there are thousands of subjects you can study in higher education, but whichever one you sign up for, the most important lesson of your university years is, perhaps, learning of languor. Languor, the pleasure of inactivity allied with the absence of pressure. 'The relaxation of yet unwearied sinews, the mind sequestered and self-regarding, the sun standing still in the heavens and the earth throbbing to our own pulse,' wrote Evelyn Waugh in *Brideshead Revisited*.

Waugh was of the opinion that languor belongs exclusively to Youth, and indeed 'dies with it'. Can languor persist into later life, or be reattained? We believe not just that it can, but that it should, *it must*; even if you have to work at it a little. But before we can consider this, we have a very different subject to contend with. A perennial curse of the Deserter. A folly. A time-thief. A right bastard.

Please do not turn the page if you are of a nervous disposition.

Keep digging for worms
Look out for armchairs
Dance with Tall Tracey from sixth form
Sauce the goose
Hide the edibles
Throb to your own pulse

WORK

'Hard work never killed anybody, but why take a chance?'

– Edgar Bergen, ventriloquist

♦ Failing an Interview ♦ First Impressionism
♦ How to Win at Email ♦ Throwing a Sickie
♦ Shirking from Home ♦ The Nap
♦ How to Avoid Promotion ♦ How to Resign
♦ The Wisdom of Ivan Osman

So you've left the loving embrace of education and its deferral of responsibility. What now? Your parents no longer expect to see you lolling around the house and raiding their fridge. They expect you to earn some money, make them proud and, mostly, bugger off. While the transition to the adult world isn't as fraught as a newborn seal's journey through shark-infested waters, it's not without its traumas. Interviews, commuting, punctuality and meetings, for instance. Or, as we think of them, the Four Horsemen of the Most Tedious Apocalypse Imaginable; an Armageddon of the soul.

Novelty may make this rite of passage seem fun at first. Indeed, work has so much going for it. There's the money, but also the sense of achievement, the socialising, the cachet. So why then, despite these goodly and incontrovertible benefits, does it feel so . . . *shit?*

It is mainly down to two reasons:

1. You have to do it
2. You have a boss

Anything you feel obliged to do is liable to darken the Deserter's mood: tax returns, chemotherapy, washing up. Why should we be forced to consider such mundanities when somewhere there stands a white horse waiting to be ridden bareback along a beach, perhaps to the Neptune Inn?

To be clear, we're talking about work here, not endeavour, not vocation. Working hard at something you enjoy is fine, if you can manage it; perhaps even good for you. Not only can it engender self-esteem, it also means you can allow yourself to slip out early and bag the best table. No, we're talking about the relentless drudgery of enforced employment: the endless weeks, the crawling years, the it's-so-dark-at-the-end-of-the-tunnel-I-didn't-even-know-it-was-a-fucking-tunnel-ness of it all. *Métro-boulot-dodo*, the French call it (tube-work-sleep), but at least they have nice lunches. In China there is growing resistance to the country's '996' culture, which semi-officially requires employees to work from 9 a.m. to 9 p.m., six days a week. Japan is the birthplace of 'karoshi', meaning death from overwork. In the US it is common for employees to receive just ten days of holiday a year.

There's no doubt about it: work is a scandal perpetrated on an international scale.

According to government statistics, in 2019/20 more than 800,000 British workers suffered from work-related stress, depression or anxiety, and the numbers are increasing. It's a barely mentioned and entirely avoidable epidemic that a four-day week could really put a dent in, and that our preference – the five-day weekend – would eradicate. Add in the stress of constantly having to manage your boss, and is it any wonder that work is often cited as the single biggest cause of what doctors call 'Irritable Bastard Syndrome'?

'Choose a job you love, and you will never have to work a day in your life,' said Confucius. But where are all these jobs that people love? Try shouting 'Hands up if you love your job!' on a commuter train at 7 a.m. on a Tuesday morning and see how many friends you make.

Do *you* love your job? Here's a simple test. On a Sunday evening, when you're collecting the washing from the back of the kitchen chairs, is there a spring in your step and a song in your heart? Do you belt out 'work in the morning' to the tune of 'Guantanamera' to yourself? Or do you find yourself wondering what it would be like to be a property magnate or an heiress? Or a footballer, a high-class prostitute, a hermit, a dog . . . Anything just so you don't have to go back to those tedious targets and deathly dull deliverables.

One of many cruel truths uttered by blunt savant Half-life came when he overheard some lads in the Wheatsheaf bemoaning the imminent return to work one Sunday night.

'Monday tomorrow,' said one of them, and the rest groaned in unison.

'It's not Mondays that are shite, love, it's your life,' said Half-life. And the young man stopped eating mid-peanut and looked up, altered.

'Who the hell are you?' he said. 'And why did you call me "love"?'

'I thought you needed cheering up,' said Half-life, helping himself to his new friend's nuts. 'Get us one in and I'll tell you where you're going wrong.'

Work, of course, steals your time, and as it is the passage of time that allows us to grow and develop, in effect, work is stealing you. Take you back. You are yours. As we've noted, no one on their deathbed ever wished they'd spent more time at work, but as it's a necessary evil for most of us, this chapter offers some simple stratagems to avoid it, or at least make it more bearable.

Failing an Interview

One of the most straightforward ways to avoid work is to not get a job in the first place. Plenty has been written about how to impress in job interviews, but nowhere can you find help on how to fail one. What if you don't want the job? What if you've been sent to the interview by some baseball-capped fourteen-year-old from the Job Centre on pain of being sanctioned? What then?

Let us imagine the scene. There you are, sitting in the sterile no man's land of a corporate reception, waiting to be met by your interlocutor. You're in shock; not only is the environment alien to you, it's possibly the first time you've worn socks in a fortnight. It's as if the revolving door you passed through was a portal to a parallel universe in which everyone appears to have something to do, for some reason. Christ, you've only been there five minutes and already you're wondering if sick leave covers interviews. Imagine if you had to go there every day? You cannot allow this to happen. You must take control of your situation.

It's human nature to want people to like us – it makes us feel valued and gives us a shot of lovely dopamine – but we must unlearn our instincts when it comes to avoiding employment. Upon entering the interview room, we suggest an opening gambit of one or all of the following:

- Sitting in the interviewer's chair
- Removing your shoes
- Lighting a cigarette

Rarely, if ever, make eye contact with your interviewer, it only encourages them. Mumbling is advised, as is sighing

heavily and looking at your watch (try tapping it, too –
particularly effective if you're not actually wearing one).

Slumping in your chair is good, but be careful with this
ploy as a slump can sometimes be taken as a sign of relaxed
confidence, which is dangerously attractive to employers.
Our job-avoidance guru, Half-life, combines a deep slump
with mournful looks towards the door and a truly startling
twitch. He hasn't had a job in twenty-five years.

If you're offered tea or coffee, always accept both and say
something like, 'Fuck, yeah! Any biscuits? Had to skip
breakfast. I'll level with you, I'm not used to being up
before noon.'

After that, due to interviewers' lack of imagination, there then follows a more or less set pattern of questions. Half-life has heard them all over the years. We record some of his responses here, for the benefit of the species.

Interviewer:	Perhaps you could start by telling me a little bit about yourself.
Half-life:	Sure. After prison I took a few years off to get my head together and get used to some new medication. My interests include gambling, sport, TV and, in particular, gambling on sport on TV.
Interviewer:	Thank you. So, I'm just going to run through a few questions . . .
Half-life:	Shoot.
Interviewer:	Would you describe yourself as a team player?
Half-life:	No.
Interviewer:	Well, let me put it another way, are you comfortable working in an environment of collegiate decision-making?
Half-life:	No.
Interviewer:	I see. What are your three favourite words?
Half-life:	Taciturn and aloof.
Interviewer:	And the third?
Half-life:	That is three.

Interviewer:	So it is. And can you describe yourself in three words?
Half-life:	I only need two – lone wolf.
Interviewer:	Right. What would you say is your biggest weakness?
Half-life:	Probably my straight talking.
Interviewer:	I'm not sure that necessarily counts as a weakness.
Half-life:	I couldn't give a toss what you think.
Interviewer:	Can you give me an example of how you plan ahead?
Half-life:	Yes, I'm going on a massive bender this weekend so can we get the medical out of the way this afternoon?
Interviewer:	Can you give an example of a time you encountered a problem at work and explain what initiative you took to overcome it?
Half-life:	Sure. I once shat myself in a meeting. The trousers had to go but I stuck a couple of leg-holes in a bin liner and still made it to Wendy's leaving do, where we got absolutely munted.
Interviewer:	Could you describe your ideal role?
Half-life:	Something stimulating, meaningful and rewarding. But until then, I'm OK to work in this shithole.

Interviewer:	Where do you see yourself in five years?
Half-life:	No longer carrying a police caution.
Interviewer:	What experience do you have that is relevant to this position?
Half-life:	How would I know? I haven't started yet.
Interviewer:	Finally, is there anything you'd like to ask me?
Half-life:	Yeah. What's the best thing for genital herpes?
Interviewer:	I meant about the company. Is there anything you'd like to know about the company and its goals?
Half-life:	[From the doorway] Certainly not.

Repeat all of the above correctly and it's likely that your interviewer will call the DWP directly and your file will be permanently marked 'Unemployable'. Your work is done.

First Impressionism

Starting a new job may well be tiresome and stressful but it also presents an opportunity that shouldn't be overlooked: a chance to shape how your co-workers see you. We call this First Impressionism – or how to make the most of moving to a new place of work.

In business schools they teach the importance of your first hundred days and even suggest that you make a hundred-day plan and share it with your new colleagues. Not only does that sound like more work, we believe you can effectively do everything you need to do to establish your standing *in your first week*.

Happy hours

On your first day it is imperative that you do not arrive at work until at least an hour after normal working hours commence. If you arrive any earlier, go for breakfast. Never apologise for your lateness. Don't even refer to it. If it is mentioned, look briefly confused and then smile – as if someone has made a joke you don't quite understand. Repeat on all five days and, hey presto, your new start time is 10 a.m. Or you'll be fired. It's win-win.

Corporate Deserter Ivan Osman took this ploy to extreme lengths, albeit inadvertently. Starting a new job on a Tuesday, he had the following Monday booked off for a funeral and then missed the Monday after that due to illness. Later in that third week, while making himself a coffee in the kitchen area, he overheard a meeting being planned for the following Monday in the adjoining cubicle, at which his presence was being mooted.

'Osman?' he heard a disembodied voice say. 'Oh, no, he doesn't do Mondays.'

Osman, alert to the opportunity, saw immediately the possibility that had been presented to him. And, sure enough, for the rest of his time at the company he worked a four-day week. He became the go-to guy for tips on long weekend European city breaks. He is currently the MD of a successful international news organisation. He still doesn't do Mondays.

Dress code

For your first week dress very – almost dementedly – smart. A top hat and tails or a ball gown, perhaps. This will mark you out as one of the eccentric upper class, which will unsettle the sort of lanyard-licking jobsworths you will now be spending all your time with. No one is going to ask a man who wears a top hat to sort out the stationery cupboard. Not in Britain.

Sunglasses can be a useful addition. Cite 'ultra-sensitive retinae due to excessive screen work' and you'll have double bubble: an excuse for not switching on your computer and a chance for forty winks.

HR vs IT

Certain theorists have it that human resources is the department to cosy up to, but this is a fallacy. Not only does nobody know what anyone in HR does, but they will always be on the side of the most senior person in the room, regardless of how many drinks you bought them the night before. Instead, immediately seek out members of IT. Information technology is now the most important department in any company that will still be around in ten years' time, so it makes sense to befriend them and build alliances.

The question 'Do our friends in IT know about this?' will allow you to stall any new development that looks like it may lead to more work. Also, they tend to have a secret beer cupboard. Worth a wander over on a Friday afternoon.

First meetings

For your first one-to-one meeting with your boss, suggest you have it on foot in your lunch hour. The message here is: you are already impossibly busy and there is no time to be wasted. Include a stop at the dry cleaners and you reveal yourself to be fastidious and demanding, particularly if you pick up dry-cleaned underwear.

If you have underlings, hold your first team meeting in a bar. These people – your team – are people who you want to do things in order to make you look good. Treat them as such. It is not enough to rely on their pathetic wages. Give them things, fun things: booze, time off, laughs. Their happiness is your happiness. Having said that, it's crucial for your standing to fire at least one of them before the end of week one.

Ensure you book in two or three external meetings, especially with suppliers located at the seaside. (If you don't have any suppliers located at the seaside, finding some that are is an essential first week exercise.) You will be spending a lot of time out of the office in the months to come and you must get everyone used to it immediately.

Deskplay

Rarely, if ever, be found at your desk. Take every opportunity to borrow an office 'to get some real work done' (thus suggesting that everyone who sits at their own desk is incapable of doing proper work) or find a spot on a different floor, perhaps at someone else's desk, where you should rearrange their photographs. This lays the foundations for later weeks when people will see your empty desk and assume you are elsewhere *actually working harder.*

Ivan Osman insists on having two desks, as far apart as possible (preferably in different buildings) and then leaves a jacket on the back of both chairs to show he is in. His colleagues always assume he's at his other desk, whereas in reality he is at the cinema.

But enough about me. What do *you* think about me?
On day five initiate, with HR, a flash '360-degree' company-wide appraisal of your efforts so far. That's right, *on a Friday*. This shows everyone how keen you are to listen and to improve. It creates a lot of positive noise about you but, crucially, everyone else does all the work. While your superiors, your team and everyone whose hand you've shaken over the last five days are all staying late to fill out those unusable intranet forms, you're sneaking out the back door for an ice cream and a lovely lean on a lamp post.

If all this sounds like a bit of an effort, you're right, it is. But implement this early work correctly and the dividends will dwarf the capital outlay. Gardeners call this kind of thing 'spadework', which is ironic because, as we shall see, when it comes to gardening this is the last thing you want to get involved in.

How to Win at Email

Let's get one thing straight immediately: email is not an instrument of urgent communication. That's what the phone is for. Despite what someone may have typed into the subject field, there is no such thing as an 'urgent' email. It's an oxymoron. Nothing that someone *might* look at, maybe after lunch, or next week, if at all, should be used to convey urgent information.

To reinforce this in the minds of your colleagues, simply do not respond to email immediately. People will come to understand that they have to wait to hear back from you and the bonus to this approach is that when you do get round to replying you will often find that the problem/request/ransom demand has been resolved.

Embrace your Out of Office auto-respond. Use it creatively. Don't just save it for holidays, put it on most of the time, so people stop emailing you. Make use of pretend departments and appointments to baffle and impress those contacting you, while simultaneously making them feel bad for bothering you. For example, at lunch you might prime your auto-respond to say something like:

I am presenting pan-departmental 2nd Quarter PCJs to FP (Regional), 1400–1700 hrs, before hosting the Make a Child Smile Charity Gala this evening. I am sure your email is important. I will respond as soon as possible.

Wow, you sound amazing. Then, if you do respond within working hours, your correspondent will actually feel flattered and impressed that you managed to get to their email early after all, ahead of the poor children.

Better still, answer emails in draft form and then fire them all off after a long dinner and a bottle of claret. Osman often schedules his emails to be sent throughout the night. His reputation is mightily enhanced.

'Pulled another all-nighter, I see,' says his line manager, as Osman wanders in around 10.30.

'Sleep is the cousin of death,' he'll shoot back, gnomically, fresh from eight solid hours of quality shut-eye.

Next up, Empty Inbox Syndrome. The pursuit of an empty Inbox is psychologically damaging behavioural folly. While you may achieve a temporary flicker of satisfaction when you delete that 'last' email, you know plenty more are following behind it and that ultimately your goal is unsustainable, a chimera.

If you yearn for the unattainable, you doom yourself to a life of disappointment. Psychologists have a term for those who engage in this sort of behaviour: fuckwits. Why not, they argue, yearn for the attainable? Like getting out of work on time.

No, enlightened email users haven't deleted an email since the late nineties. Why would you? You never know when you might need it. Just let them sit there, waiting to be rediscovered years later when you need to prove you were right about something.

Sure, your IT department will send you regular requests to delete your email due to 'server space restrictions', or some such nonsense. Simply reply to your friends in IT, 'Please stop sending me these emails as they are clogging up my system,' adding, 'If you need to discuss this matter further please call me.' No one in IT has ever called anyone.

Throwing a Sickie

Sick leave is not just a right, it is a duty. Why face the daily plague of trains, meetings and deadlines when one simple phone call can leave you alone in bed with the iPad until opening time?

Many don't take full advantage of this windfall because they fear detection or harbour some kind of conscience. In this section we offer some road-tested tips that will allow you at least two weeks' additional leave, to do with what you choose, including, of course, nothing.

The details
One sure way to stop any further questioning of your condition is to give lurid details of symptoms, especially those involving bodily functions. No employer wants to

hear about your stool, or lack of it. Offering to send a picture is not just courteous but will bring the conversation to a swift end.

For women with a male boss, any menstrual minutiae will see him off. You can even make up body parts safe in the knowledge he will erase from his mind the 'abject pustules on your swollen phalaxia' before he's even hung up.

Timing

Everybody knows that no one has really been sick on a Friday or Monday since the Industrial Revolution. It's obvious you're just trying to extend the weekend, so mix it up a bit. Call in on Thursday, then take the Friday too. If you think you've been rumbled, take one extra day you don't even want, let alone need. Attack is the best form of defence. And attack.

Forward planning

Seed your sickie by reporting to anyone who'll listen that your partner has come down with some life-sapping lurgy in the days leading up to your absence, while chuckling distastefully at his or her symptoms. This will invite 'serves them right' office gossip about you and cement their belief in your own poorliness.

The voice

Do you have a 'poor you' sick voice you put on when calling the boss? Well, ditch it. You're not calling your mother, so remember, it's not sympathy you're after, it's acquiescence. Pick a quiet room and speak calmly and firmly until you are granted your freedom. Do not, as the Dulwich Raider once made the mistake of doing, phone in sick from a sunny terrace overlooking the Royal Ramsgate Marina. Not when you live in south London.

'Is that . . . seagulls I can hear?' asked his boss.

'*Seagulls?* I wish,' he laughed. 'If only!' But he knew the game was up.

Thinking outside the pox

Whatever you may call your occasional bouts of sniffles – a cold, flu, the Widowmaker – unless it's full-blown coronavirus, bosses will grow weary of it as an excuse. So flus and colds have to be used sparingly and interspersed with explosive gastrointestinal incidents, car crashes and sick children (if you don't have any, invent one at the interview stage – it makes you seem grown up and, played well, will offer endless excuses for time off). Think ahead and collect medical equipment such as neck braces, eye patches and arm slings for later use.

Above all, keep it simple: 'I'm sick – honestly, you

don't want to know the details' is surprisingly effective in deterring further enquiry.

Shirking from Home

Once simply the place where we slept, ate and argued with family, the home is now, we're sorry to say, also becoming a theatre of work. In some ways, this could be considered a step forward. You're not in the office, for a start. Not only can no one hear you scream, no one can see you skive. Save your screaming for the office.

But one ubiquitous technological development, accelerated by the response of businesses worldwide to Covid-19, threatens the status of the home as your private sanctuary and erodes that feeling of aloneness that makes being at home during the day so special. We are referring to video conferencing.

Left untamed, Zoom, Teams, Hangouts and the like can be a disaster for the modern shirker. Not only are you expected to join conference calls at a moment's notice, but now you have to actually dress for them as well, at least above the waist.

Our Roxy played a blinder on this one. Spotting this encroaching danger early, she not only complained bitterly to anyone who would listen about her (non-existent) 'intermittent home broadband issue', she also actually wrote to her local MP about it and sent a screenshot of the response – complete with Houses of Parliament letterhead – to her boss, with a furious note asking if she could somehow intervene. Now, when she is working from home, her boss knows not to bother her with requests for video meetings, lest she is again asked to get involved in lengthy correspondence with our legislators. A reminder that bosses, too, are often keen on the path of least resistance.

Talking of bosses, Ivan Osman's 'Zoom in the Room' gambit – in which he brings a gravitas to his team meetings by gracing them with his virtual presence – is worth a mention. It's a simple enough ploy to utilise Zoom's background facility to show a scene of, say, your study, even though you may be on the beach. That's entry level. But Osman takes this one step further by using a background image of his home office *with him actually in the picture*, sitting at his computer, looking directly at the camera.

His brooding, unmoving on-screen presence, giving his staff the silent treatment, has dramatically upped the problem-solving abilities and productivity of his department, while he's in the kitchen eating hot buttered crumpets.

As ever, Osman has a slightly different take on Teams

and other collaborative work tools. He loves them. By judicious flicking between various statuses on his phone ('Busy', 'Be right back', 'In a meeting', 'Fuck off' and, every once in a while, 'Available', for example) he is able to give the impression of a man hard at it, day and night, wherever he may be; the digital equivalent of his two jackets ploy.

'Keep the collaboration to a minimum. Especially with bosses. They're always after something,' he confides. 'I carry in my pocket the facility to always be "working" even when I'm on the golf course or a nine-day cruise to Singapore with my mother.'

Of course, if you work for yourself, working from home is already one glorious orgy of tea, biscuits, YouTube, masturbation and snoozing. Well done. But for the ordinary corporate employee, what was once a much-cherished opportunity for some me-time on the payroll is in danger of being ruined by log-in checks, keystroke monitoring and Trigger-happy Tina in marketing setting up another meeting to approve keyring designs. No, these days, it's probably safer to do your napping at work.

The Nap

Can there be anything more exhausting than getting up and going to work? Is it any wonder that you arrive ready to collapse, what with our blighted transport infrastructure, the pissing rain and staying up late to watch the poker? The answer, of course, is to top up on sleep at work.

Our sleep specialist is the Dulwich Raider, whose special talent is not simply the ability to feel sleepy in any given situation, but to act upon it. The Raider has proudly napped at every job it has ever been his misfortune to hold. We are indebted to his work in this area.

If you're lucky enough to have a storeroom or similar at your place of employment it might be possible to create an area hidden from common view, an approach known as 'nesting'. The Raider once worked in a carpet store, for example, where he was able to arrange the upright rolls in such a way as to create a reasonably complex labyrinth, in the middle of which he had concealed an old armchair and a footstool. He would eat his lunch there and follow it up with forty winks, covered in crumbs.

And in the warehouse store of a large hospital, he once removed – at enormous physical expense to himself – all the individual boxes from a large container of Corn Flakes, into which he was then able to climb for some downtime whenever the need arose. This worked perfectly until the day he was awoken by an unfamiliar sense of weightlessness as he was forklifted across the warehouse floor. He emerged, blinking, and was fired without even being given the chance to properly wake up.

For nesting to really work, though, you need a lock and key. In times of extreme sleep deprivation, a locked door is your friend. Indeed, the Raider reports that for a time the mere sound of a key turning in any lock would render him heavy-lidded. And so, the simplest answer to work-sleep prayers is – as if you didn't already know – the toilet. The blessed place where, finally, you are alone with your thoughts and your habits, however horrific.

One source of disappointment for the weary worker is the toilet cubicle in which, due to a ghastly design oversight, the door doesn't quite reach the ground. While the seated snooze is still possible here, it is safer to avoid the floor. During an attempt at some deck action in one such toilet, the Raider's feet were spotted peeping out from beneath the door by security. He was able to convince them that he had fainted during a particularly gruelling evacuation attempt. Fortunately, there was no comeback from the incident and he went on to represent the company at the highest level.

Much better is the wholly discrete cubicle, with full-length door and, ideally, a low-slung cistern. The presence of the latter allows one to practise the 'reverse cistern gambit'. In this manoeuvre one straddles the bowl, lid down, facing the cistern. Remove the toilet roll from the holder and place it on top of the cistern in front of you. Then simply lean forward (slump, if preferred), using said toilet roll as a pillow. You can even give the cistern a little cuddle, if you like. It's nice to give something back.

But the ultimate nap zone, the very Jerusalem of the office siesta, is the disabled toilet; preferably the one in the basement where no disabled people can actually get to. Its size and spaciousness allow for a full-length horizontal experience that can be rivalled only by some-how obtaining the keys to that office penthouse apart-ment that you keep hearing about, but that in all proba-bility doesn't exist.

Furthermore, disabled toilets rarely come with fore-shortened doors, which we suspect is due to the unwrit-ten rule that while it's just about acceptable for your boss to peek under a toilet door to see if you're in there, to do so to a disabled person would be considered the MO of a tyrant.

How to Avoid Promotion

Ivan Osman claims that the higher up an organisation you go, the less there is to do. 'Or, at least, you can do it all over lunch.' And while this may be true in many workplaces, for the truly lazy there are also dangers in promotion. Eleva-tion can bring about scrutiny, or worse, responsibility. And who wants to be responsible for anything other than the TV remote?

Sure, a bit more money is nice, but promotion can lead to an end of the quiet life and uncomfortable questions about your whereabouts and how you spend your day, like it's suddenly everyone's business. The indolent must protect the vagueness of their precise location until it's time to knock off.

Climbing the career ladder can bring terrible demands on your time. You will be asked to attend meetings at an hour when you should be considering a set breakfast. You'd think incompetence would be enough to avoid it, but you only have to look at politicians to know that failure does little harm to employment prospects.

Worse, in the real world, poor performance can get you the sack. In these heady days of efficiency savings and wanton productivity, there's always a bean counter looking for a knighthood by cutting staff to the bone. Ordinarily, being made redundant would be a bonus, what with that lovely pay-off and the sheer breadth of on-demand TV. But what if you've got mouths to feed? You simply can't allow yourself and your butler to go hungry. Here are some ideas for clinging to that job but avoiding promotion.

Do nothing
Show willing, but complete as little work as possible. Be the master of the pending project. Delegate upwards. Volunteer for nothing. If you must go to meetings, make sure you don't contribute in any way that might mark you out as someone with their finger on anything other than the biscuits. To our knowledge, Dirty South holds the record

for attending the most consecutive work meetings without saying a word, at fifteen. At the sixteenth, though, he was asked the direct question, 'What is it that you actually do?' and two weeks later he was fired, so there is jeopardy in playing completely dumb.

'Mind you, if I hadn't been sacked I might never have taken Dulwich Hamlet to the finals of the Champion's League in *Football Manager*,' he recalls. 'So, swings and tings.'

Be invisible

Keep your head down and be at one with your surroundings, like a zen carpet. Blend in, so that when promotions or redundancies come around, yours is the last name anyone remembers. Consider changing your name bi-annually to throw them off the scent and keep you off lists.

Go big

Former havens of the work-shy – the nationalised industries, councils, the Civil Service, etc. – have been trimmed down to become lean machines mostly devoid of comfy, indefinable positions where the slacker might find salaried peace.

Once, you could remain undetected in an entry-level government-funded gig for a lifetime, doing very little while complaining about your heavy load and massive pension. Now, you're expected to work for it, as if you weren't an actual princess, like your mama said you were. Now, perhaps, only vast multi-nationals are big enough for people to get lost in. The bigger the company, the better the chances of the endless lunch for the picaresque hero.

Spanish icon Carlos Recio showed us all the way during his tenure in Valencia's provincial government, where he earned €50,000 a year while doing precisely nothing. For ten years, he clocked in at his office at 7.30 a.m. before heading out, only returning at 4 p.m. to clock out.

'I've been working like a dog,' he claimed, though investigators were unable to discover any record of work he had done during the entire decade prior to his sacking in 2018. But his crown has been usurped by a hospital employee in Italy who has been accused of skipping work on full pay for fifteen years. Instead of being given a medal he is now being investigated for fraud, extortion and abuse of office. Legend is an overused word today, yet here it seems barely sufficient.

Little Dirty South

It's a difficult balancing act, doing just enough to keep your job, but little enough to avoid being noticed. The tightrope is fraught with danger, as Dirty South found in his early years.

Before he took up job-dodging full-time, the Dirty one was a work-shy schoolboy. Immediately after failing his

GCSEs, he decided to take a gap year for as long as possible. After a summer of watching Test cricket and nicking the old man's booze, he was told to get a job or get out. Or at least leave the gin unmolested.

A largely fictitious CV landed him a role at a market research company where he took up smoking for the hourly breaks that came with it and became a national expert on recommended rests from computer screens for health and safety reasons. It was a crap job, but he grew to love the fags.

Staff turnover was high, and so after sticking it out for six months, he was the longest-serving prole in the company. He was called in to the office and asked by the boss how he would fancy stepping up to supervisor, with responsibility for an entire team of two. He was too young and naive simply to refuse.

He left the meeting distraught. Desperate for an out, he deliberately walked into the corner of a staff locker. He collapsed to the ground, rubbing his eye into the cheap carpet to redden his face, and faked unconsciousness by cunningly shutting his eyes and muttering, 'Possible concussion.'

The boss insisted on escorting him to the hospital, where he was obliged to continue the charade. Forced to spend the night on a ward, and still pretending to be unconscious, he was enraptured by the tender touch of the night nurse.

He made a miraculous recovery when the breakfast trolley appeared and returned to his duties after a suitable period of sick leave, as if nothing had happened. Promotion was never mentioned again and he retired, penniless, at nineteen, but with a lifelong nurse-based peccadillo.

He subsequently attempted retirement several times, whenever he was threatened with progress, until he finally achieved unemployability. His early experiences taught him that advancement lurks around every corner and must be faced with determined deviousness and extreme evasion. 'There's an army of wonks out there trying to get you to take work seriously, to grow up and get on, the work wonk wankers.'

How to Resign

There is one working day that every Deserter looks forward to; the culmination of all your dreams and plans. You've seen the lucky ones go before you and now, finally, it's your time to shine – you are about to resign.

Conventional wisdom tells you not to burn your bridges, but don't let conventional wisdom spoil your big day. When has conventional wisdom ever bought you a Fanta? We advise you to douse those bridges with petrol and strap dynamite to them, before lighting the pyre of your career with a spliff the size of a lightsabre. Going back is bad. Like driving in reverse, in a mad sort of way.

There are three main options to consider:

The disappear

Some consider this a cowardly option, but then they probably regard cowardice as a negative thing, rather than the noblest of human virtues. If faced with insurmountable odds, nick off and put your feet up, isn't it? Don't stand there and fight like some sort of idiot.

And so, if you have to face an intimidating boss with the news that you're not only leaving, but that the work you were supposed to have done is in such a shitstate that it will take a miracle to unravel, do the decent thing: leave a note and bugger off. This does have the disadvantage of you not being present to see your boss going purple with rage, but it also means no working your notice period. Go immediately to your sofa for a well-earned rest and a noodle on Netflix.

You can say things in writing that you'd never muster in person. You can be rude, angry, gleeful, or even Welsh. You can also tell the truth – 'Somehow I lost the burning passion for logistics that I mentioned at the interview stage.' Plus, if you mention your boss's sexual proclivities in a resignation letter, you can be sure it will never reach HR and your departure will be accepted without question.

The graceful exit

Maybe you're just too nice to insult people and feel the need to restrain yourself from a wholehearted celebration of your good fortune. In this instance, just gradually rub it in that you are going on to a better place. Follow a dignified resignation by doing less work each day until all you're using work for is the Internet and toilet paper. Start wearing sandals. Then shorts. Then swimwear.

Avoid any further proper work by making a big song and dance about your 'handover document'. Spend an inordinate amount of time on it, including such attention to detail as best local, finest all-day breakfast and nearest place for a lie-down.

Come into work every day singing a happy song at the top of your voice. Have the biggest leaving drinks in the world and snog everybody. After all, no matter what you say about staying in touch, you will never see them again and only fancied them because they sat near you and every day got more beautiful, like a cellmate.

The nuclear option

As exciting as it is waiting in your boss's office with your naked butt in the air ready to offer an unmistakable resignation with your fundament, unless you're a contortionist you're again likely to miss out on seeing the horrified look on their face.

A face-to-face, expletive-filled verbal rant detailing your boss's shortcomings is generally the way to go and is wonderfully cathartic, as long as you don't have to return to say: 'By that, I meant a pig-eyed arse-nugget who writes generous references.'

But sometimes an awful job or boss deserves the fiendishly creative resignation, with an audience and a flourish. Journalist Stephen Pollard leads the field with his parting column for the *Daily Express*. Camouflaged amid a workaday piece about the farming industry, Pollard used the first letter of each paragraph to spell out 'FUCK YOU DESMOND', for the benefit of the *Express*'s then proprietor, Richard Desmond. Not only did it form an exemplary acrostic resignation, it also cost him a job at *The Times*, who revoked their job offer to him as a result. Losing two jobs for the price of one is state-of-the-art Deserting. Hats off.

Your email account will stay active for a good while after you leave so use your out of office to leave a personal message about the company. For example:

I have now left the company. Please email Simon if you would like a simple enquiry turned into a catastrophuck, Marianne if you're happy to wait until next year for an answer or Tobias if you enjoy condescension from a chinless, red-trousered oxygen-thief.

Leaving drinks

Never hold your leaving drinks before your last day. There is nothing to be gained from coming back into work the day after you let off the fire extinguishers and carved your initials into the boss's door.

Dirty South's favourite leaving drinks were at a rather conservative media company. One of his colleagues was a part-time stripper who after a few, taught all the other girls how to instantly remove a bra with just two fingers. They were all at it, precipitating a mass bra-swap, leaving one woman in a bra two sizes too small for her, at least according to conventional wisdom.

The gang then went on to Moses Never Closes to snort ketamine off a library card and swim in the carpet. Dirts had such a good time he went back to work for them six months later so he could have another leaving bash.

The goodbye email

Get your message across under cover of apparent manners: 'My two years at Slog & Perish have taught me a great deal, not least about swipe cards and the benefits of booking meeting rooms in advance. And I can honestly say, hand on heart, that I would rather have been here with you guys than with the finest minds in the business.'

Memories
Not all work experiences are bad, and it's important to remember the positives in the avalanche of negatives. When the Dulwich Raider left one post, he photographed his favourite toilet, where he had spent so many happy hours. He keeps it on his desk at home, along with all the stationery he liberated from the clutches of capitalism.

The Wisdom of Ivan Osman

Osman has his own particular view of work, being, as he is, rather good at it.

On returning to his native Midlands after university, he took a year off to dabble in art and magic mushrooms, but when he got fed up painting the inside of his mind (and being skint) he set about crafting dozens of CVs featuring non-existent work experience and unexpected skillsets. (The truth was he'd never picked up a bow and arrow, let alone been crowned Three Counties

Longbow Champion four years running.) These he fired off to various organisations and within a year he had talked himself into a nice gig in London's Soho. He was off.

As he rose through the ranks of a number of national and international media companies he was surprised, as noted previously, to discover that the higher he got, the less actual work there was to do.

There were early mornings, difficult bosses and endless laundry, but as long as he delegated effectively and knocked together some adequate presentations, he found that work can in fact be excellent cover for a life of long lunches, Internet day trading and boozy jollies – most of the things that he'd be doing anyway, except now he was being paid for it.

For him, work is the 'ultimate skive' – not to mention a crucial component in his plan to get rich quick and retire at forty-five. He has kindly allowed us to present here some of his notes on the matter, which he plans to collate into an international business bestseller, provisionally entitled *How to Win at Work: 99 Habits of the Highly Successful*.

Dedication: For my children – here is what I've learned about how to amuse yourself, climb the career ladder, become vastly overpaid and retire early.

- Everything you think you know about work is wrong. Far from being something to fear or avoid, it is a game to be played. And, what is more, it is a game that can be won.

- Corporations are giant bolt-holes full of money, liquor and food, with toilets perfect for sleeping, fucking & doing drugs in.

- 90 per cent of success is showing up. The rest is down to pretending to work.

- There will be obstacles. There will be mistakes. There will be doubters. But one thing there will never be is commitment.

- Whatever you do, don't be yourself. Be the person they think you are.

- Be sure to have your hangovers on work time. Your own time is for installing them.

- Take your lunch hour out of the office and return with your lunch, to eat at your desk. This makes you look busy. Use your actual lunch hour for drinking and sex.

- A dream does not become reality through magic; it takes bribery, sycophancy and blackmail.

- Be prepared to agree with idiots if they pay your wages.

- Meetings are where you tell people to do your work – and in front of everyone else, so there is no comeback.

- Never overtly disagree with someone in a meeting. Simply say, 'Maybe we should take a step back here.' And then restate your position, but this time standing up and shouting.

- Cancelling a meeting doesn't make people sad, it makes them happy. If your staff need cheering up, arrange a meeting and then cancel it.

- Make personal telephone calls in a glass-walled meeting room to look busy and important.

- If you do actually have work to do, do it in the boardroom. Then, when you're turfed out, you'll be seen as busy by all the right people.

- The P&L is everything. Literally stop at nothing to avoid using negative numbers.

- When preparing a presentation, if you can't make the P exceed the L, don't prepare the presentation.

- Never present a graph of anything going down. It makes people sad. Especially bosses.

- Never book half days off. Every day is a half day if you just piss off.

- Is that 99 yet?

So there goes Osman, driven to earn as much as possible, as fast as possible, so he can retire as early as possible. That way he will have the time and money to splash out on the things that give his life meaning, such as his children. Along with strong cider, archery and a couple of au pairs to look after the children.

How different this is to the approach of Dirty South, for whom retirement is too reminiscent of religion, in which you have your reward in some unimaginable, unverifiable future. He advocates retiring immediately after education, while you're young and able to enjoy it, borrowing hard, maxing out the credit cards and paying all the debt forward to your elderly self, too frail and addled to answer back as you are forced to get your first job aged fifty.

As we shall see in 'Money', the answer perhaps lies somewhere between the two extremes. But before that, let us leave the world of work, thank God, and turn to those things that make life worth living.

Ride a white horse
It's not Mondays that are shite, it's your life
Make it to Wendy's leaving do
Yearn for the attainable
Straddle the bowl
Do it all over lunch
Nick off and put your feet up

LEISURE

'The end of labour is to gain leisure.'

– Aristotle, philosopher

♦ How to Do Fuck All ♦ Psychogeography ♦ Holidays
♦ The Art of Lunch ♦ Relaxation ♦ Sport ♦ Booze

In so-called civilised, complex societies, it is perhaps no surprise that leisure – time away from work, chores or study – has traditionally been a privilege of the wealthy. After all, without consigning 98 per cent of the population to work for them, how are the 2 per cent expected to become wealthy in the first place? What is perhaps more surprising is that anthropologists have discovered that the more simple the society, the more leisure time its people are afforded. Which has an interesting effect on their lives: they are happier.

When our gregarious Mancunian friend Spider found himself burned out by a demanding job, he decided to take a sabbatical and spend some time in Africa to recharge his batteries. Here, inspired by a book he'd found beneath a leg of a wonky coffee table at Dirty South's flat, he sought out the Dobe !Kung, a hunter/gatherer bush people from the Kalahari Desert, Botswana.

The !Kung, he discovered, only spent around four hours a day on the hunting and gathering. The rest of the time they spent – as we might call it – messing about.

Someone would light the fire for a barbecue and they'd gather to tell stories, sing, dance and play games.

'I'd never seen so many smiles in my life,' says Spider, who stayed with them for some months. 'And I became convinced there was a direct correlation with their lifestyle. These people were loving life. And they didn't even have Sky Sports. I felt that in the West we'd got our priorities all wrong.'

What might we infer from this experience? We are not suggesting that we all become hunter/gatherers – most of us are not yet ready to wring the necks of Henny Penny for the Sunday roast, not with a hangover – but it does suggest we need to be mindful that our work/leisure balance may be skewed and unhealthy, and that we might be happier working less and playing more.

In the last chapter we discussed how we might make work bearable and free up some time for ourselves, but in order to get the most out of leisure we may need to unlearn some bad habits. It is vital, firstly, that we understand that leisure time is not to be frittered away willy-nilly, like work time. Time is not money. It's better than that. It's time. And yet it is remarkable that many of us are unsure how to spend free time wisely, maybe because, regrettably, leisure has been omitted from the national curriculum. The provision of a simple module on how to enjoy it could be the greatest breakthrough in governance since the founding of the National Health Service. And yet it falls to us to offer advice on how to use this most precious time of all, with all its pleasures and pitfalls, benches and comfy sofas.

So let us make a start. And remember: a journey of a thousand miles begins with staring out of the window for a bit.

How to Do Fuck All

Recently a fascinating research paper came to our attention entitled 'Doing Nothing and Nothing to Do: The Hidden Value of Empty Time and Boredom'. It is almost as if the author, Dr Kets De Vries (INSEAD, Fontaine-bleau), has been watching over our shoulders and tapping into our philosophy and stratagems.

In the paper he suggests that doing nothing is crucial to the creative process and that, far from being a waste of time, introspection and reflection induce states of mind that nurture our imagination. Our obsession with 'keeping busy', he postulates, not only suppresses our true feelings and concerns, but also the means by which we may deal with and solve them. Must our day be filled with schedules, deadlines and tasks? No sooner is one task completed than another grows, like a starfish with chores instead of limbs. Hideous.

He has a pop at mindfulness – that modern way of relieving anxiety by taking time out to 'feel the moment' – suggesting that working manically all day and then squeezing in a mindfulness session between your last conference call and squash with Simon in sales is a 'Band-Aid' solution that doesn't address root causes of stress or unhappiness. Sod being busy, he implores, try doing fuck all for a bit (though not, to be fair, in those exact words).

We're bound to say this is quite go-ahead advice, coming as it does from one of Europe's leading business schools, where the business of work is taken very seriously indeed, according to our man in the know. (The Dulwich Raider lived in Fontainebleau for a while and dated a toothy INSEAD bilingual translator from Chipping Sodbury. She never knew that he actually lived in a tent in the forest.)

We've long since appreciated the benefits of doing nowt. Apart from De Vries's observations above, it's so much less *tiring* than getting things done. And it can also bring its own sense of achievement. The Raider reports that during A-level revision he sat in his kitchen for hours, preferring to watch the clock than to return to his books in the next room. So intently did he watch it that not only could he clearly see the minute hand going round, *he could discern movement in the hour hand*. Not everyone will be lucky enough to experience this kind of pointless wonder – that takes a special kind of dedication to doing nothing, something that the demands of the modern world conspire to preclude.

So, what is to blame for this obsession with 'always on' busyness, and how can we combat it?

Connected devices are a big problem in this regard. Look around you at the café, on the train or waiting for a bus ... Everyone's on a smartphone. Even your friends in the pub. Perhaps especially your friends in the pub. What are they all *doing*? Mainly creating emails, tweets, posts, messages and updates. Yes, we're all complicit in maintaining the busy-busy illusion. Remember when we used to just gaze into the middle distance? The world still twirled and, more importantly, we had time for a natter or to mentally work through important issues, like whatever happened to Tall Tracey in sixth form.

Could the online tasks being sold to us – and creating value for tech companies – actually be . . . *more work*? Work masquerading as leisure activity? Or at least, do such digital dealings blur the lines so that we no longer really know when work stops and fun starts? That WhatsApp group, that dating app, Facebook, Twitter, LinkedIn . . . they seem to compel us to contribute and respond, and so we do, because we have convinced ourselves that we need to keep up, to be connected.

Remember that day when you forgot your phone? Do you recall how the initial frustration gradually, hour by hour, gave way to an unfamiliar sense of liberation? Hang on a minute, you realised, I'm on my own, like the old days. I'm untrackable. I could *go to the Wheatsheaf*. One old friend who lost his phone was so delighted to discover he loved not having one that he decided not to replace it. (Sadly, we don't see him any more. Can't get hold of him.)

The need for speed is another culprit in the 'busyfication' of our lives. The commendable Cittaslow movement, founded in 1999 by a group of Italians who (probably) hadn't quite finished lunch, aims to improve quality of life by slowing down the pace of existence in whole towns and cities. By slowing down you may not get as much done in the short term, but you might find yourself a whole lot happier doing it. And it's really not hard to implement. Don't take the car, for example, take a bus. Don't take

76

the bus, walk. Don't walk, amble. Don't amble, lean.

Do you really need to be in Paris from London in two hours? For half the price of the train ticket you could instead take the coach and treat yourself to a nine-hour journey with free wifi, electricity *and* toilets, which would allow you to revel in the very act of travelling as well as enjoy your destination. (This strategy is not unreservedly recommended for trips with new partners, and is to be avoided altogether for anniversaries and honeymoons, unless you wish to travel alone.)

As Dirty South discovered, taking up smoking may help in your attempts to slow down. Science has it that smokers are addicted to nicotine but, in fact, many are simply addicted to just getting out of the room, away from *les autres*, to stand by a road and look at the traffic for a bit. Why not buy a pack of cigarettes and give yourself some time out? You don't even have to light them.

However, those tempted to take action – or, rather, take no action – to get less into their lives should proceed with caution. Your other half may not like this new you. It takes a truly enlightened partner to respond with a cheery 'OK, love!' when you say you can't unload the dishwasher because you've decided to do fuck all for a bit, or that you missed the shopping delivery because you were lying on the chaise longue 'watching the trees'. There is the distinct danger that what you are doing could be construed less as a scientific experiment and more as the kind of hopeless vapidity that gets people excluded from the gene pool.

Nevertheless, having finished Dr Kets De Vries's paper we decided, in the interests of research, to set our inactivity expert, the Dulwich Raider, a task: a day doing nothing. Nothing at all.

His report follows.

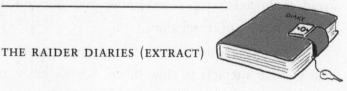

THE RAIDER DIARIES (EXTRACT)

9 a.m. Wake up.

10.30 a.m. Wake up again. Reach for my phone and remember I've left it in my desk drawer downstairs, where it is to remain all day. Look at ceiling for a bit.

Get up and take a shower. Ah, the shower! A place where you can't have phones anyway, where there is no TV nor anything, really, to do. You can just lather up and stand there like a plant in the rain. A great start.

11 a.m. I dress myself, but without thinking too much about it as I don't want it to constitute doing something. I go downstairs, put on the kettle and stare at the dog while I wait for it (the kettle, not the dog) to boil. This

is the same dog that I recently caught lolling her head out of her basket so she could take a drink from her bowl without actually getting up. Today we are on the same wavelength.

I look at the drawer in which my phone lies, alone. The computer sits on the desk above it, cold. I'm going to have to get out of here. I grab my keys and my hat and say my goodbyes.

'You've got your shirt on inside out,' points out Mrs Raider.

Walking is good for nothing, if you see what I mean. You're not just alone with your thoughts, but are also able to enjoy the stimulation of passing scenery together with the low-level thrill of your own rudimentary motor skills. Running would almost certainly count as doing something, but walking is almost like breathing.

Every now and again I try to take stock of what I am thinking about, to see if I am freeing up my subconscious to resolve problems in my absence, but it's like trying to catch your shadow. The main thing I seem to be thinking is, 'I wonder where I'm going?'

That soon becomes clear.

12.30 p.m. I arrive at my favourite café and give my subconscious a hearty pat on the back.

I order egg, bacon and chips. The place does a good

breakfast but it does feature the ubiquitous frozen chip. Why, I wonder, almost aloud, don't more cafés offer fresh chips? I immediately reprimand myself for thinking about something useful. Then I decide that thinking is not actually doing, so thinking about chips is probably OK, as long as I don't actually go looking for fresh chips, or, worse, attempt to make them.

Christ, this could be a long day.

My food arrives. Momentarily, I worry whether eating is actually doing something. Who would have thought my day would throw up so many philosophical questions? I reassure myself that eating can't really count as doing something, for if I didn't eat, then there would be no me to do anything, let alone something, or indeed nothing. I eat.

Fortified, I head into Brixton. I have no specific destination in mind but, rather, I am just letting myself be led by my feelings and surroundings. When it starts to rain though, pretty soon my feelings are drenched and I duck into the covered market for a coffee and a wander. I'm not shopping. I'm mindlessly passing shopfronts, which is nothing.

2.30 p.m. Is drinking beer doing nothing? This is a question I wrestle with as I walk up the high street. Because if it is, I could drop into that new place that is supposed to do great ale.

But the question is academic because when I arrive, it's closed. I wonder what time it opens. I decide to wait. It might be an hour. It might be three. Whatever. I take a seat at an outside table on the pretty tree-covered forecourt.

This is doing nothing, alright.

Lovely nothing.

God, the Sainsbury's opposite has got big signage. The apostrophe alone is the size of a man's head. Ridiculous. But now a more pressing issue forces its way into my consciousness. One of imminent lower intestinal evacuation. When is this gaff going to open for crying out loud? How long am I expected to sit here, alone among the leaves and the spiders?

It's no good. Oversized sign or not, I'm taking a dump in Saino's.

3.15 p.m. The last time I took a dump without any decent reading material was in 1997. I can still tell you everything you need to know about Silkience shampoo and conditioner, including that the conditioner, in a remarkable scientific breakthrough, 'only goes where it needs to go'. I should remember it; I read the label seven times.

Now I don't even have that luxury, as I sit listening to my own intermittent breathing. Worse, I'm not even in Sainsbury's, I'm in McDonald's. Despite having a store sign only slightly less obtrusive than the Shard, the

Sainsbury's doesn't even offer lavs. How did that get through planning? I make a mental note to add this to my list of complaints about the retailing giant.

I emerge from McDonald's into the hurly-burly of the high street. Ah, people. That's what I need. Where can I find people?

3.45 p.m. One thing you can be sure of with a Wetherspoon's is folk, and Brixton's is no exception. On my arrival it's already half-full and most of the punters seem to be my idle brethren. Old boys sitting alone, nursing a pint, staring at the wall. Are they happy? Chilled out?

'What are you fucking looking at?' says one of them.

I buy a pint and take a table of my own. After some moments gazing out into the busy street I find myself thinking about the tax benefits of an offset mortgage. WTF? If these are my daydreams, I do not wish to be alone with them.

I reflect on my day. Have I solved any ills? Have I given myself creative impetus? Have I de-stressed? What I have certainly learned is that doing fuck all, all day, is tough and that by the end of it you will really need a pint and some company.

As if on cue, Half-life arrives.

'Alright?' he nods. 'What you been up to?'

'Nothing,' I reply, honestly, and explain my day's mission. 'What do you do when you want some proper down time?' I ask him.

'I have a woman who comes round for some smack action,' he replies.

'Wow. Spanking?'

'Something like that. Listen, I've got to drop off a package for Strange Martin. Get us one in.'

Instead of doing nothing, I think to myself, maybe I should find some new friends.

Having considered the Raider's struggles with doing nothing, we are tempted to conclude that perhaps it is easier to do nothing when you actually have something to do. That is, having something you feel obliged to do makes doing nothing more desirable and enjoyable. Like the Raider when he was supposed to be revising. The moral of the story is: set yourself free by finding something to do and then not doing it.

Psychogeography

Unbeknownst to him, what the Raider was engaged in on his day out was psychogeography, a pursuit that provides hours of happy accidents, healthy strolling and a thoroughly undeserved sense of respectability. Psychogeography means leaving maps behind, following your instincts and getting lost in a city to rediscover the thrill of not knowing what's next.

The father of psychogeography was the Situationist theorist Guy Debord, who in 1950s Paris embarked on a series of playful urban wanders, guided by his subconscious response to the architecture and geography around him. He called these unplanned journeys *dérives*, or drifts. Cynics would call them pub crawls. As, presumably, did Madame Debord.

Situationists contended that even in an era of advanced capitalism and technological efficiency the worker still only functions with the goal of survival. And that the purpose for which capitalism is organised isn't luxury, happiness or freedom, but production. The production of commodities is an end to itself, and yet never ends. All of which makes it pretty tough to get even an afternoon on your tod. So off Guy would go on his wanders.

Drifting changed the way Debord saw Paris and, consequently, felt it also changed him. He was a weighty intellectual; a philosopher and filmmaker who attached great significance and meaning to getting lost. He believed that by veering off the predictable path your eyes are opened and you develop a new awareness of your surroundings. He abhorred what he called 'the spectacle' of consumerism, which values commodity and image over authenticity and directs us to adopt prompted desires. He urged us to follow our own compass, to slip off the end of the herd and down the track that lacks a signpost but may harbour unexpected pleasures, like a giant beanstalk or a tiny bar. Debord's drifts were often carried out with a sympathetic friend and involved numerous cafés they just happened to drift into, directed by the 'psycho-geographical contours . . . currents . . . and vortexes' of the city and, possibly, happy hour.

Given his highbrow credentials, it is comforting to discover that Debord came across the practice of drifting not in a dusty attic while scratching his chin in silent contemplation, but by smoking hashish in a park and getting too stoned to find his way out. Instead of seeking help he explored, seeing the place anew. And when he arrived home much later than expected, with the raging munchies, he could legitimately claim he'd been working late.

'Home honey, I'm high!'

'*Quelle heure* do you call this?'

'*Alors, je travaille sur une nouvelle théorie révolutionnaire.*'

'Pfff.'

Getting lost in your home city can make you feel like you're seeing it for the first time. It is a simple way of becoming excited again, just like in those halcyon days before you knew what a tax return was. While it may be true that a good drift begins and ends in a bar, there is intrinsic value in the aimless wander. You end up seeing your city's ignored corners. And in a flexible state of mind, the unnoticed can be remarkable.

We should add that the *dérive* requires a city to stroll in; a dynamic hub of human activity. Drifting in the countryside could go horribly wrong, leaving you in the awkward company of beasts of the field, or, worse, people from the next village. The drift requires a certain density of buildings, along with no specific destination, the potential for surprise and the likelihood of licensed premises. Otherwise, you're on what is known as 'a walk'.

Equipment is vitally important for a successful drift. There is none. Unless you count shoes as equipment. What you don't need is a bag of any kind, as it will mark you out as an amateur and see you ridiculed by *flâneurs*, Situationists and Reificationists. Especially the Reificationists. You can forget about Google Maps, too. What is the point of getting lost if you can instantly locate yourself and be directed to the safety of the nearest Chicken Cottage?

So if you're ever drawn to try a road simply because it has an odd name, or feel inexplicably called to mysterious alleys, maybe there's a psychogeographer inside you, whimpering to get out. Or maybe you're drunk, in which case it is the perfect time to start drifting.

Roxy on tour

When Roxy's on-off Dutch boyfriend, Jan, wanted to visit a famous London landmark, she reluctantly agreed. But she made him promise to join her for a non-specific wander in Thamesmead the following week as a quid pro quo. Even he had to admit it was more fun. And he's an idiot.

A Visit to the London Eye	
The London Eye is a big wheel next to the River Thames.	
1. Buy £30 ticket. 2. Stand in queue for forty-five minutes. 3. Get frisked by security. 4. Board pod with strangers in which drinking or smoking is prohibited despite nice views. 5. See if you can spot Auntie Dave's house. 6. Look out of other side of the pod for a bit.	7. Fiddle about with the multi-media offering. 8. Think about how thirty quid could have paid for a nice lunch. 9. Alight and join heaving throng of tourists back on Earth. 10. Buy a fridge magnet with a photo of you looking the wrong way on it for £14.95.

A Thamesmead *Dérive*

Thamesmead is a suburb in south-east London built as a social housing experiment in the 1960s.

1. Choose starting point: Lesnes Abbey, Abbey Wood.
2. Get lost in ancient woods looking for abbey.
3. Walk over bridge into Brutalist housing estate and experience living museum of what the future used to look like.
4. Discover horses tethered in communal estate gardens. Pat them, feed them, ride them bareback.
5. Stroll beside waterways and enormous lakes. Point out a submerged Vespa.
6. Spot grebe and lapwing at Crossness Nature Reserve.
7. Marvel at the Victorian Romanesque glory of Bazalgette's pump house at the sewage treatment works.
8. Discover the location of *Thunderbird 4* – on top of a shed outside a factory – and simply know the world is a safer place.
9. Discover a river (the Thames again), smoke a Blue Peter and take a riverside walk.
10. Find downtown Thamesmead and stop by the canal to feed crisps to ducks and have a drink in a caged beer garden once owned by darts legend Andy Fordham.

Final score: Thamesmead 10, London Eye 0

Holidays

If there's one thing we have learned from the coronavirus pandemic, it's that people love holidays. Millions of people were in lockdown to avoid a debilitating and deadly virus, but the day-to-day hot topic was *When are we going to get back to Torremolinos?* It's almost as if, for most people, holidays are more important than life. This becomes a more understandable – and forgivable – position when you consider that, for many, holidays *are* life. Those other bits – the getting up, going to work, paying the bills, cooking, cleaning, childminding (also known as parenting) – really aren't up to much. The holiday is the best bit. Maybe the only bit worth having.

And it's not hard to see why. A holiday is when people get to do just what they want for a bit, including nothing. Sleep in. Have a fried breakfast. Have another ice cream. Overdo it on the sun lounger. It's up to you. You're on your 'olidies.

We wouldn't wish to deny anyone such simple pleasures, but our aim is to make our everyday lives a little bit more like a holiday, one day, one hour at a time, even if it has to be only in your mind. An additional day off a week – or even leaving work early – can make all the difference. Imagine not crawling into work on a Monday, but spending the day improving your mind, or indeed slightly worsening it. (It's up to you. You're on your 'olidies.)

The gig economy may have forced down overall wages, but it does at least offer you the chance of reducing your hours. Failing that, walks, long lunch hours or spells alone (or, indeed, accompanied) in the bathroom all not only snatch back a bit of your time, but also a bit of your life, enabling you to maintain a sense of volition and thereby a sense of self. Holidays, we insist, are not just for the holidays.

'When I "work from home" in the summer,' says Roxy, 'I just head to a different part of town with the laptop, so it's all new and feels a bit different. Then I slap on the Ambre Solaire and take a two-hour lunch.'

The Art of Lunch

The daily helter-skelter of modernity is such that even the simplest of pleasures must now be filched as if you were an outlaw and wolfed down like you're famished. Or planned in advance like we're all project managers or something. Subsequently one of the day's most obvious gratifications, lunch – the first meal of the day – is more often than not reduced to the ritual chunneling of baguette into your gullet while sitting at a desk or queueing at the post office.

We have lost sight of one of mankind's greatest inventions: the long lunch.

Look at the numbers: the average lunch break taken in the UK is thirty minutes. In France they get two hours. That's right, while we're champing on their pallid *batons* they're settling down to fine wines and four courses. In Spain they even have a little sleep afterwards. When did we get so backward?

Lunch, put simply, is the reward for mornings; our appetite the return for getting out of bed. Done properly, it is a respite from life's rigours; a mini holiday, if you like. It is a mystery why we have allowed the extended midday meal to slip from our consciousness, combining as it does three of our favourite things: eating, drinking and not working.

Pass the menu and let's consider some of the elements of this lost art.

Starters

The long lunch requires friends, trusted colleagues or people you fancy – preferably a combination of all three.

Ideally, you will want nothing from your lunch companions and they will want nothing from you. This leaves you free to discuss the breadsticks, gossip about fellow diners and expound your theory that, due to global warming, greenhouses will soon be as rare as the Cockney sparrow, which may ironically precipitate the latter's return as aphids will once again be readily available . . . Conversations of the gods.

If you're unlucky, someone will postulate that a lack of aphids is more likely due to their monophagous desire for sap under negative hydrostatic pressure rather than the presence of greenhouses, at which point just smile and reintroduce the subject of breadsticks. It's important not to get too bogged down in detail.

Mains

Does the food matter? Experts (or similar) are divided.

Corporate Deserter Osman insists on the finest cuisine known to humankind, but that's OK because he's buying it on his gargantuan expense account. Dirty South, on the other hand, is fine with anything as long as he's heard of it, it doesn't come from the sea, isn't greens and is in fact pie and chips.

We're somewhere in between. If we're going to invest a couple of hours of our lives somewhere, we'd like the food to be reasonably interesting and not too expensive. We don't want our pleasure reduced by worrying about the bill. As we shall see, conserving funds is an important consideration. And anyway, we haven't ordered the wine yet.

Drink is a crucial component of the long lunch. The ordering of wine must never be in doubt, notwithstanding a refreshing lager beer or an enlivening spirit to commence proceedings. Wine oils the conversation: it helps secrets to be told, plans to be hatched, breadsticks to be interesting.

Dessert(er)

The lunches of which we speak should not be taken in those 'one hour' places, where they will 'need the table back' or worse, actually close at some point and try to run you off the premises with the stench of bleach. The long lunch requires a minimum of two hours, with gaps between courses, much mulling, chats with the waiters about sparrows and a little something to try from Chef. It's at this point that Osman will usually send his subordinates back to the office, to fight the good fight, while he orders a dozen oysters for pudding.

What happens next is up to you. We consider post-lunch an opportunity for a kind of Situationist liberation, a *flâneurie*, in which whims and fancies overrule traditional afternoon activities and so-called 'requirements'.

It only takes one person to say, *Well, to be honest, there's nothing I actually need to rush back for* and suddenly a new path for the day unrolls before you, like your own personal red carpet. Some may decide to order another bottle and stay put awhile, some may even go for the ultimate goal of remaining in the restaurant for so long you eventually order dinner. Others may yearn for cocktails, and suggest a little place they know round the corner with an excellent two for one deal. By four o'clock you'll be raising blue drinks and bellowing Situationist slogans like 'Free the passions!', '*Ne travaillez jamais!*' and 'Anyone fancy a game of darts?'

As for the settling of the bill, splitting payment is all very well (and, of course, fair enough) but it hardly needs saying that in an ideal world someone else will be doing the paying. Lunch extremist Half-life is expert at instigating the freebie – he claims the last time he paid for one was on a date with Grace Jones in 2001. Should you happen to mention that you won thirty quid on your acca at the weekend, for example, his face will light up in conspiratorial glee.

'You fucking genius, you should celebrate!' he'll say, softening you up before adding, 'How about lunch?' Next thing

94

you know you're stuffed to the gills, £60 down and sharing a twilight spliff by some bins. But, man, does it feel good.

Relaxation

So, making the space to unwind mentally is a fine use of one's leisure time and can bring great benefits in terms of inducing calm and freeing your mind. But it's not just your mind that needs a little holiday; at the end of a short day the body, too, yearns for peace and the visceral thrill of soft furnishings.

The sofa

Once upon a time, somewhere between the Big Bang and the Chesterfield, there was a world without sofas. People sat upright, alone. If they wanted to pass the nachos, they'd have to get up, sighing at their burden, maybe even swearing.

The Ancient Romans had their couches or *lecti* to recline on while slaves pushed grapes into them, but the grape-slave function wasn't enough to keep the sofa relevant throughout the Dark Ages. When the Roman Empire declined and fell, sofas went the way of underfloor heating and the vomitorium. But in late seventeenth-century France, a revolution in furniture design occurred. Suddenly seats were made for multiple persons, with upholstery for comfort. Without a division between them, people could now sit next to each other. French people.

Soon, every Tom, Dick and Henri wanted a sofa. They became the must-have item of the time, replacing the ubiquitous bidet in the affections of the wealthy. People filled their houses with sofas, the loons, as if the armchair never happened. Sofas represented the rebirth of relaxation for a continent ready to put its feet up.

Along with the sofa came a new attitude: a freer, lounging kind of vibe. The writer and politician Horace Walpole gleefully described the experience of reclining on a sofa as like 'lolling in mortal sin' – which is all the invitation we need to pay homage to the humble settee. You can understand why it took so long to invent the cathode ray tube or internal combustion engine, but comfortable seating? A species that values the development of the musket over the couch is one that needs a stern talking-to.

Sofas went very quickly from something for two or more people to sit on, to something for one person to sprawl on. The previously vertical French court became fashionably horizontal, to the alarm of uptight, upright traditionalists. Sofas developed further, becoming more comfortable and versatile as humans evolved into slouchers. They became the focus of the home, the place where everything happens. Sex, pizza, everything.

The sofa is a truer reflection of the soul than the oft-cited eye, or less-oft-cited knitwear. Some prefer to retain the formality and elegance of the Jacobean period, living in show-home perfection, unsullied by family life. Others use it to store loose change, foodstuffs and mice. The Dulwich Raider's mother used it to conceal the empties.

The sofa supports all kinds of human activity, and indeed those of other organisms: it's like an ecosystem with cushions. It's a friend that requires nothing in return, unlike many of our friends. It represents humanity's acceptance that there is something more to life than the daily grind. Not life after death, but *life during life*. Because for all the awfulness of a day at work – and for all the fun we have going out to play – at some point we will come home. To the sofa.

And yet, can there be such a thing as too much comfort? A life on the sofa, like a life on the sea, has its hazards. While it's easier to avoid scurvy, the disappointing truth is that a completely sedentary life is not good for you. If only there was a way in which you could relax and exercise at the same time. To, if you will, relaxercise.

Leaning
Before soft furnishings there was leaning, invented by the English in the seventeenth century, around the same time as public houses, non-coincidentally. And thus the atavistic

urge to lighten your load by placing an elbow on a surface around breast height and look around you for a bit resides within us all.

Look at today's pub-goers, for example, who gather outside certain hostelries across the land. Elbows up, legs a-cocked, stance slanted . . . No one taught them this. *It is pure instinct.* And a perfect way to relax body and mind. Not to mention get some fresh air and take on board some life-giving fluids.

Some places are better for leaning than others. Simply leaning against a wall or a door at home may invite opprobrium. The mantelpiece is the ideal domestic leaning station, or at a push, the kitchen island. When in town, seek lamp posts, while it is the simple five-bar gate that offers the country alternative.

Tune out. Turn off. Lean on.

Sport

In nineteenth-century Britain, opportunities for organised leisure pursuits increased as wages grew and hours declined, after a series of Factory Acts reduced hours worked from ten, to nine, and then eight hours a day. This is still some distance from our demand for the five-day weekend, of course, but at the time it was revolutionary. As a result, participation in all sorts of sports increased and interest in spectator sports in particular grew dramatically. Games were organised, rules were formalised and sports like cricket, football and rugby developed passionate and devoted followings.

Today, as then, spectator sport allows us to project our desires and ambitions, often without leaving the aforementioned sofa. We imbue teams and individuals with characteristics we hope reflect who we are and what we represent. Our sports stars save us from having to perform strenuous exercise, cut down on the sauce or buy mock-Tudor property. We take the reflected glory of victory, but are free to walk down the street unhindered by clamorous fans.

Yet there is more to the enjoyment of sport than winning, knee slides and hugging strangers. It allows us to spend our free time in excitement, anticipation and celebration. It embraces our love of games, which is itself related to the wise use of time. Time, especially leisure time, is not for killing, it is to be savoured, like the sun on your back or a bar of Cadbury's Fruit & Nut when the kids are out.

Some sports take little time. Boxing, for example, can be thrilling but over in seconds, as Dirty South recalls, having paid a fortune for a ringside seat at a bout that lasted less than half a minute. 'It reminded me of the night I lost my virginity,' he reflects. 'All that anticipation, momentary explosive action, then coming round with smelling salts.'

But few things are as delightful as sport that goes on for hours, or even days – unless we're participating, in which case we'll be needing a lie-down and some fluids. Cricket and horse racing are long-form, consumption-led spectacles which only require as much attention as you are willing to give. They are specifically designed for the time-rich: the retired, the unemployed, the sicknoters, the Deserters.

Meanwhile, football offers camaraderie and an inevitable visit to a hostelry, so it's 2–0 up already. And who can ignore that little frisson of excitement you get when you see that Everton are away to Tromsø in the Europa League and kick-off is at 4 p.m., hopefully with an orange ball?

Sport is, put simply, the opportunity to play, and who would turn that down? Here are a few ideas to help you feel like a winner.

Football

While the beautiful game is endlessly fascinating to play, its suitability as a day out for spectators – at least at the higher levels – has been marred by inflated ticket prices, the sense that winning is the only thing that matters and, worst of all, drinking in the stands being banned under Football Association rules.

While you may not get the vast crowds or sense of national import at the lower levels of the game, non-league football provides an antidote to this gradual ruination by offering a renewed sense of fellowship, local adventure and a return to the sheer fun of mankind's struggle with an inflated bladder. Why spend a whole day and hundreds of pounds traipsing round EPL grounds when football, beer and a sing-song is right on your doorstep?

Temporarily set aside your other loyalties and for ninety glorious minutes you are all in it together. What's more, you don't have to decide until half an hour before kick-off. Just see how the day unfolds and leave at the last minute with a cheery 'Ta-ta!' to loved ones. Why not lighten your partner's load by taking the kids? It's an ideal opportunity to trial parenting by benign negligence.

Children run free around non-league grounds, seeking you out only to ponce a pound for some crisps. And whether you're berating a lino or throwing your pint in the air in the event of a goal, they enjoy seeing grown-ups being interesting, for once.

Cricket

A Test match can go on for five days. That's five days of sitting around drinking, eating and hoping – at home, in a pub, or at the venue. Five days that are punctuated by moments of genuine joy and excitement, as wickets fall, thunderous sixes are struck, or a pigeon lands on a helmet.

There are so many reasons to love this ponderous, gentle, eccentric pursuit. There are ten ways to get out. They stop for tea. There are endless impenetrable figures and infographics. At Canterbury, home of Kent Cricket, they had special laws to accommodate a twenty-seven-metre lime tree on the field of play, so that you couldn't be caught out if the ball struck it. When, after 200 years, the tree was given only another ten years to live, they planted another in the ground and obtained permission from the cricket authorities to move it to the pitch when the original lime met its demise. Sadly, when that day came earlier than expected, the sapling was too small to be a nuisance and so remained outside the boundary ropes. But how can anyone not love a sport that harbours such respect for botany?

Cricket, for the uninitiated, is basically institutionalised dissing, with stats. You throw a ball at someone and if they miss it, they are a twat. If they hit it, you are a twat. If the ball smashes their wicket or they hit it into someone's hands, they're a wanker. Then it's time for lunch.

The batsman's job is to repel the bowler, or humiliate him by losing his ball in the crowd. The bowler is equally determined to embarrass the batsman. The only thing that equates to that feeling you get when you've followed the line of the ball, moved your feet and affected a firm defensive posture with the bat, only to hear the clattering of stumps behind you, is thinking you have enough time to get to a public toilet and finding you don't.

The upper hand can pass from team to team in sudden decisive moments, but mostly, it's the gradual drip, drip, drip of clever, patient batting or bowling that wins the day. Meanwhile, you can have a sandwich, stick on your Out of Office and watch the Internet. But we believe the live game is even better and persuaded our non-cricket-loving chum Half-life to overcome his concerns that it's the preserve of autistic toffs and join us for the day.

The kick-off in cricket is usually at 11 a.m., so will often require an alarm, or lateness. We know which one we prefer. We were deeply encouraged to read on our ticket: 'Spectators may not bring more than 4 cans/1 bottle of wine'. It felt like an order to BYOB. And when you run out of booze, there are two or three bars to keep you going. Half-life had four cans of Guinness in his bag and several more strapped to his legs, giving his gait the suggestion of injury. Thus unfriskable, he was waved through.

At some grounds, you can wander round the pitch with your drinks and sit down pretty much anywhere, though you need to pick your spot for a smoke-up. We found ourselves not wholly focusing on the match until Half-life sparked a blunt. Suddenly the pace of the game fitted ours and we settled into some seats, mesmerised by the unfolding drama. Although drama is perhaps not the word. It's a little like European cinema – ponderously slow and then, just as you are wondering what the fuss is all about, taking you by surprise with sudden violence: a swing of a bat, skittled stumps or a curiously spinning orb coming straight at you.

The vibe bore no relation to noisier sports we're more familiar with. The crowd clapped good play from both sides and harboured no resentment toward their victorious opponents. Kids played on the outfield at lunch. Lager was not the drink of choice (ale was), and we were not alone in drinking all day, which made a pleasant change.

'My people!' roared Half-life, when it erroneously

dawned on him that he could be in like-minded company. But they started to back away or look at their shoes to avoid the gaze of an erratic giant.

England gave the world football, cricket and rugby, which is remarkable in itself considering we're often so poor at them on the international stage. But unlike the other two, cricket is all skill and cunning, which makes it special. And then there's the sledging:

'Why are you so fat, mate?' an Aussie bowler once asked of Zimbabwe's rotund batsman, Eddo Brandes.

'Because every time I shag your wife, she gives me a biscuit,' came the reply.

Over!

Horse racing

Racing is tailor-made for a stolen day. There is almost certainly a racecourse near enough to allow you, in theory, to leave and return home at the usual time, as if you were going to work. Apart from the slurred speech, Guinness stains and pockets full of betting slips, no one will be any the wiser. It's no coincidence that race-goers call races 'Meetings'. Next time you see '2 p.m., Meeting' in a colleague's work diary, think of this: he's not at Tamara's PR debrief at all, he's having the time of his life, flopping his wad on the nags at Ascot.

The magic begins as soon as you board the train to the course – the train, you may recall, going the other way. Here, gradually, you will spot the first signs that you are not alone: a *Racing Post* here, a tweed cap there, someone with a tin of gin and tonic and an actual pair of binoculars ... These are people preparing for a day out of the ordinary, a day getting away from it all, a day, in short, at the races.

At the course there is a simple repeating pattern of pint, paddock, pick and punt before watching your chosen horse trail in, last. At least, it's simple at first, but gets increasingly challenging as the day goes on. But nothing can detract from the pleasures of a day skiving in the country air: daytime drinking, stats, gambling, shouting and consuming mainly beige foodstuffs. You can even wear a funny hat. What better way to stick it to The Man?

Fishing

Some may consider fishing a natural pastime of the likes of us. It has many of the hallmarks of the lifestyle we crave: sitting down, getting away from it all, tinnies, waterside daydreaming, Scotch eggs. There are, however, an awful lot of rules about how and what you can catch (clubs and dynamite are discouraged, for instance), a lot of cumbersome equipment that threatens the easy country stroll and the possibility that you may have to pay actual money for maggots.

Then there's the photography. You, grinning like a hick, sporting rubber footwear and holding up your reluctant prize, boasting to the world you have outwitted a beast with the IQ of a pebble. It's not a high point when a simple fish is embarrassed to be seen with you in public.

We prefer a kind of fishing tourism. Merely sit near someone else's rod and do everything an angler does, except the angling. A splendid way to spend a sunny spring afternoon, with no licence or lake fees, plus you can move to another spot if you fancy, with no tiresome packing up or freeing quarry from a bucket in the hope of gratitude. You can even vicariously experience the thrill of the catch through your 'host angler', cheering them on with helpful information when they land something: 'Fish! Fish! It's some kind of fish!'

As the Raider is fond of saying: 'Carpe diem', which he

claims is rendered in some translations as, 'Seize the carp!' Not perhaps the meaning most are familiar with, but if it leads to a riverside meander and snacks, who are we to argue?

Booze

The consumption of alcohol has, for many of us, become an essential part of our leisure time. Evenings and weekends are synonymous with casting aside the rigours of existence and getting right on it. We use it to celebrate, to console ourselves and to fill in the long, lonely days between celebration and consolation.

It makes our friends seem interesting, it makes us repeat ourselves, it leads to bus stop cuddles and it makes us repeat ourselves. Some people even have it with dinner! But where did it come from, this liquid that fends off reality, makes us feel good, look good and changes our notion of what a very good idea is late at night?

A potted history
Gods often get the credit for inventing alcohol-based recreation. Like Bacchus, the Greek god of wine and copping off. Or Radegast, who, according to Slavic legend, invented beer in his role as god of hospitality. However,

Slavic religious beliefs have only been handed down orally, as they were unable to write, which suggests an admirable devotion to Radegast's alleged creation.

Flemish cultural hero Gambrinus is also credited with inventing beer, but then he is also renowned for drinking vast quantities of the stuff, so possibly the two stories became conflated over time.

'What, that pisshead there?'

'Yeah. Reckons he *invented* beer.'

'Get out.'

'Oh yeah. And chips.'

In fact, it was a happy accident. In certain conditions, yeast breaks down the natural sugars in fruit or grain to produce ethanol, a type of alcohol. The nice type. And yeast can be found in the air, so we didn't even have to muck about with test tubes to discover the magic of fermentation. It's a naturally occurring process that predates humans. We just noticed it and then harnessed it in order to make people laugh at our jokes.

For most of our existence we have been hunter-gatherers, chasing our food around the countryside and picking fruit, nuts and berries in small nomadic groups, like prehistoric herberts. Then, during the Neolithic era, a proto-Deserter fancied a nice sit-down. We stopped running hither and thither. Especially thither. We paused, we grew stuff and instead of chasing animals, we put up fences to keep them in, which also gave us somewhere handy to lean when we mastered growing cereal and discovered beer.

We were off. Beer was soon being brewed in Egypt, Babylon, Mexico and Sudan. It became so ubiquitous and so popular that it formed part of labourers' pay. Those who built the Great Pyramids in Egypt, for example, were provided with a daily ration of a gallon of ale that clocked in at around 5 per cent ABV. Tell that to your boss next time you slip off your chair after lunch.

Pubs

> 'There is nothing which has yet been contrived by man, by which so much happiness is produced as by a good tavern or inn.'
>
> – Samuel Johnson

No discussion of leisure could be complete without considering the public house. Indeed, many leisure activities implicitly include pubs in their modus operandi, even if they remain unspoken. A long country walk, for example, a trip to the seaside or a sporting occasion. Even a mention of a night at the theatre or a visit to an art gallery will evoke thoughts of the pub in the experienced tactician, who will have committed to memory the locations of the best ones in the vicinity of almost every public attraction.

The pub. That institution peculiar to our lands; the oasis in the desert; the lit window in the gloom; the building that, let's face it, makes a street actually mean something. It's difficult to put your finger on what it is that makes pubs so lovely, so sought after – indeed, so world-famous. It's as if you'd need several fingers, which is ridiculous. But one key element is the offer of respite from the day-to-day bedlam of life (although some of the ones Half-life frequents contain quite enough bedlam of their own).

You might visit when you seek company, but also when you wish to be alone. They are places in which lively conversation and quiet contemplation are equally welcome. In which not only can we physically leave behind, however momentarily, the pressing issues of our lives – of the world – but are also encouraged to holiday our minds through the use of a liquid-based intoxicant. Just seconds after it's on the lips, it's in the brain, parcelling up our cares and posting them to tomorrow like a demented mailman of the psyche.

Pubs are a refuge and, crucially, one in which there is nothing in particular to do. Contrary to most other public or quasi-public spaces, you are actually encouraged to loiter. And as seminal French film director and layabout Jean Renoir reminds us, 'All great civilisations have been based on loitering. ... Think of the Greeks, for instance. ... What were the Greeks doing in the agora? Loitering. ... The result is Plato.'

In 1946, George Orwell, in an effort to put off writing the follow-up to *Animal Farm,* wrote an essay for the *London Evening Standard* called 'The Moon Under Water', in which he considered the various elements that might coalesce to create the perfect pub. They were as follows:

- Victorian architecture.
- Games in the public bar.
- Quiet enough to talk, with no radio or piano.
- The barmaids know your name.
- Tobacco, aspirins and stamps for sale – and they will let you use the telephone.
- A 'snack counter' with cheese, pickles, mussels and liver-sausage sandwiches.
- Table dining upstairs.
- Draught stout.
- Glasses with handles.
- A large garden.

That doesn't sound too shabby, does it? Even viewed from a different century. It is as if the requirements are timeless. Indeed, if you'd been fortunate enough to enjoy an ale all the way back in the seventeenth century, perhaps from a pewter pot in the Severed Head, beneath the boiled bonces of traitors at the southern end of old London Bridge, the interiors and the general atmosphere may not have been substantially different from that of today's classic local.

Unless it was quiz night.

Quiz night

One's enjoyment of a pub can be impaired by poor-quality beer, perhaps, or by loud music or TV. Maybe even by bad lighting or a grumpy landlord. But there is one thing that is sure to kill it stone dead: quiz night.

We've all been there. You've arranged to meet some mates for a catch-up about how brilliant everything is, you push open the pub door and immediately a sixth sense – some vestige of animal instinct, perhaps, still intact despite years of neglect – tries to tell you something. As usual, you ignore it.

You stride purposefully over to the bar, eyeing the punters hunched over their tables and wondering what it is that the hushed atmosphere reminds you of . . . That's it, it feels a bit like *work*. Weird.

'What's going on?' you enquire of the barman as he pours you a golden pint.

'Quiz night,' says the barman.

'Oh, for fuck's sake,' you say.

'Shhh!' says someone next to you holding a tiny pencil.

Quiz night? It's our old friend: work masquerading as leisure. If we'd wanted to have people shout questions at us from another room we'd have stayed at home with the family. Pubs are for chatting, for meeting strangers. Pubs are for jokes, for taking the mick, for discovering stuff, for forgetting other stuff. They are to recover from work, to put your life in order, to share problems and ideas. They are to set yourself adrift on the ebb and flow of random topics, for the concatenation of dreams. But no, you're stuck in a room with forty know-it-alls who need an excuse to go to a pub and then, when they do get in one, sit there in silence trying to remember all the venues of the Winter Olympics since 1924.

You mustn't break the vow of silence to call the gang to warn them, oh no, and so you text them instead.

'Er . . . excuse me? No phones allowed,' hisses an earnest geek in a roll-neck jumper, emboldened by being with his people.

'It's alright, I'm not doing the quiz,' you smile back, politely, and he gives you a look.

'Oh, really?' he persists. 'What are you doing on your phone, then?'

'I'm texting your mother to tell her you're a twat,' you say, and he looks a little hurt.

At length your mates pitch up, and on the way to the next pub – any pub – you remember why they're your mates.

'Thing I can't stand about quizzes is that they either involve showing off, which I don't like, or watching other people show off, which I detest,' says Dirts.

'While either being laughed at for being stupid or laughing at someone else for being stupid,' says Roxy.

'And if I was going to do one, I certainly wouldn't do it with you thick cunts,' says Half-life, proving that given the choice between a quiz night and conversation, one should always choose conversation: it's so much easier to win.

Micropubs

Recently pubs have been closing at an alarming rate, mostly as freeholders realise the land value and sell up to developers so they can be turned into overpriced flats with pinched balconies and views of other flats. What is wrong with these people? They obviously don't like pubs, which suggests some sort of genetic deficiency of the soul, so perhaps we shouldn't be too hard on them. But why do they have to inflict their shortcomings on the rest of us?

Thankfully, this trend doesn't tell the whole story, for we are also in the midst of a pub revolution: behold the micropub.

Micropubs – tiny, one-room boozers in which mobile phones are nailed to the wall and asking for lager is a criminal offence punishable by stern tutting – are popping up throughout this blessed land. High street shops (back-street shops even) previously without hope or hop are being converted into small rooms offering ale, pork pies and conversation, a bit like the kitchen at parties.

It's one of those ideas, like takeaways or the snooze button, that seems so blindingly obvious once it's happened that you can't imagine how no one had thought of it before, and for it we have to thank Parliament (yeah, really) and a certain man of Kent.

A chance encounter with a local licensing officer gave Martyn Hillier, a florist from Herne, in Kent, an idea. The Licensing Act 2003 (which came into play two years later) changed the permissible objections to licensed premises. The days of big breweries preventing competition through perpetual legal action against anyone fool-hardy enough to want to run a bar were over. Now anyone could open a pub.

So that's what Hillier did.

In 2005 the Butcher's Arms opened in the old butcher's shop, with twelve seats, pickled onions and some of the finest local ales in the county. It was an instant hit and won CAMRA's East Kent pub of the year. Twice.

Hillier wasn't finished there. Filled with evangelistic

fervour and a love of his fellow drinker, in 2009 he gave a fifteen-minute presentation at CAMRA's AGM in Eastbourne on how to start your own micropub. The result was a beer-fuelled revolution – quite the best kind, in our view.

Attendees of that meeting started micropubs as far afield as Hartlepool and Newark, but it was in Hillier's home county of Kent where something akin to magic occurred. Within months, micropubs had opened in Ramsgate, Margate and Westgate-on-Sea; within a year they were in Deal, Broadstairs and Folkestone. And now they flourish throughout the country: not far off a thousand, at the last count.

Over the years, during extensive research, we've found that the best pub in town is often the smallest, and micropubs tap into this phenomenon. Many are 'one-conversation' rooms, where everyone joins in with whatever is the topic of the moment – like how pubs used to be before breweries took them over, built an extension, stuck on the telly and turned up the music. (Then were able to sell them off because they 'weren't working'.)

One criticism is that micropubs tend to be very male-dominated. We've found that women are warmly welcomed into every one of them we've been to, but there is the sense of a reclamation of lost masculine spaces, like working men's clubs. Roxy did see a sign in the lavatory of one Kentish micropub that read, 'Will women please return the toilet seat to the upright position when they have finished.'

'The "please" had been struck through with marker pen,' she recalls. 'Bless their little pot bellies.'

Parklife

You wouldn't be human if you didn't look over at bench-drinking park hobos and wonder where your life went wrong. Look at them, cackling and fighting and enjoying the fresh air. Not for them the daily travails of alarm clocks, ablutions and achievement. I mean, you don't need to clean your teeth if you haven't got any, right?

While the advent of Covid-19 was a disappointment in many ways (bankruptcies, destitution, death, etc.) it did give us all the chance to experience such parklife for ourselves. With the 'Pub Pox' or Great Closure of 20/21, we were forced to re-evaluate fields and parks. And we discovered they are not just for flying kites and a go on the swings, fun as that is, but can also be social destinations. Almost overnight we were buying camping chairs, swigging beer from milk cartons, pissing in the bushes and living wild with the down and outs. You might say we *were* the down and outs, and we bloody loved it.

A spot of fresh air, tunes playing over Bluetooth magic, smoking whatever you want, when you want . . . There is a lot to like. And it's so much cheaper. For the price of a couple of pints of craft IPA you can pick up a slab of lager from Saino's that will make you a hero. It's probably terrible, but it is a slab: little wonder that some of us have never gone back.

'It made me realise that life isn't just about drinking in pubs; it's also about drinking outside,' says the Raider. 'That's why camping chairs come with a netted aperture in the arm. Possibly the single greatest invention since the camping chair itself.'

The microbinge

There are times, sadly, when your day is so filled with arseache, you don't want to get out of bed. Our advice is: don't. There are other days, however, when this is not an option; days filled with obligation in which there is so little wiggle room, you have to make every gyration count. Like when you have to appear sober at both ends of the day. We know. Nightmare.

This is precisely why Dirty South invented the microbinge (not to be confused with a micropub, though it may well involve them). With its requirement for planning and forethought, the microbinge is proof that Deserting is not passive, go with the flow hedonism. It involves actively putting yourself in the path of pleasure's potential. You may be slacking, but not because you don't care. Quite the opposite.

It all started with the Dirty one having to drop the nipper off first thing and pick him up at the end of the day. It looked like a day without colour: work, lunch, more work, childcare. What is that about? How about: a little work, pint, spliff, pint, pint, power nap and recovery? This would give him a few hours in which to play, then regroup and return smelling of roses, as opposed to hops, tobacco and girls.

The problem with any binge is that it tends towards a loss of control. One drink inevitably leads to another and you could end up spending the night in the first skip you pass that contains a mattress. Lovely, but not the level of self-awareness the ideal candidate for the microbinge will possess.

The key is to work backwards. If you have to deal with sober, serious types at 5 p.m., you need to start your hangover around 2.30. That's just science.

Like all great inventors, Dirty South wasn't aware he was embarking on a pioneering journey. He just got restless after working at home for an hour or so. He needed fresh air and a walk to clear his mind and become productive again. So he strolled to a nice spot next to a pond. Sitting on a bench with his paper and pen it wasn't long until he realised he needed a table. About five minutes, to be precise, at which point he noticed it was midday.

Where can I find a table?, he asked himself. *Where can I find a table at opening time?* Luckily, such is the randomness of the universe, he was writing on his knees not thirty seconds from one of his favourite hostelries.

'I've only come in for a table,' he told the barkeep. He seemed to understand. 'Do you have anything that goes well with a table?' he enquired.

The barman recommended a session pale ale. Perfect. At 3.8 per cent you could chug down a couple and still be able to fly a plane. A few more and he'd be ready to nick one. He started to feel magnificent again.

He even did some work on the table, though some would call it merely crossing stuff out. He had immovable appointments, but still needed one more push into the creative hotspot. He skinned up a little feller knowing that, if he employed the sort of iron will that made this country great, it would be his first and last smoke of the day. Suddenly he couldn't stop writing. Sadly, it didn't do much for his handwriting and he would later need GCHQ to decipher it.

Satisfied that he had achieved both some decent work and had a facking lovely time, he celebrated with another pint, some grub, and another pint. Next, the hard work would begin. He made his way home to begin the process of restoration. The fuzzy parts of his mind needed to be rebooted, despite the inevitable calling to his very soul for more of everything.

First, the power nap. Twenty minutes of glory and a harsh wake-up. *Is this what being in the army is like?* he pondered when he awoke, cross, confused and ready to invade a rogue nation. Strong coffee, bitter dark chocolate and a ten-minute lie-down in a warm tub full of pink Alpine crystal salts he found in the cupboard saw him wave goodbye to the shores of intemperance. Estimated time of sobriety, 4.58. He had arrived at his destination.

It was only when he spoke to proper grown-ups that he got that sense of 'they know what I've been up to', despite his functioning perfectly well and smelling like a Swiss stripper. All paranoia disappeared though at the sight of his little'un running towards him, arms outstretched.

'Did you have a nice day?' Dirty South asked him on the walk back.

'Yes,' he said.

'What did you do?'

'Nothing.'

'Attaboy.'

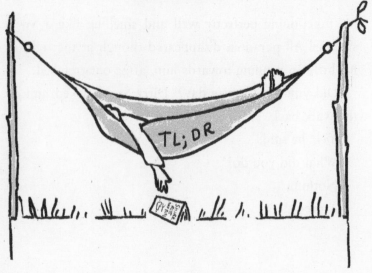

Stare out of a window
Live in a tent in the forest
Slip off the end of the herd
Talk about breadsticks
Lean on
Stop for tea
Wear a funny hat
Loiter like the Ancient Greeks
Find something that goes with a table

HOME

'If I were asked to name the chief benefit of the house,
I should say: the house shelters daydreaming.'

– Gaston Bachelard, philosopher

♦ Home Office ♦ DIY ♦ Housework ♦ The Garden
♦ Shopping ♦ Family ♦ Coping with Christmas

For Laura Ingles Wilder, author of *Little House on the Prairie*, home was 'the nicest word there is', though she wasn't a big pub-goer it's true. Warm cornbread was probably the closest she came to experiencing euphoria. Home was once where the heart was, the place for communal meals and sharing stories. Then along came broadband and suddenly we could all be on our own devices; all together, all alone, at home. But now our cities are filled with wifi'd caffeine palaces, with their charming baristas and courgette muffins, so what, in this modern world, is the home for?

Like pubs, the home should provide an escape from life's pressures. It should be somewhere that invites relaxation and peace. A place in which your desires reign, should you live alone, or at least have some dominion, if you don't. Home is where the only rules are your rules. The place where you can put your feet up, scoff a tub of ice cream and watch any old tosh, without the judgement of others. Should the Queen of England knock at your door, you are perfectly within your rights to say, 'No,

Betty! You *cannot* enter, for this is *my* home and *Corrie*'s about to start.' Unless she's carrying a curry and a bottle of splosh, in which case she's almost certainly welcome.

The role of the home is to provide an undisturbed realm, yet the path to peace is littered with obstacles.

Home Office

As discussed in 'Work', the home has become an arena of industry, especially since the pandemic when all the bosses who swore working from home should be forbidden suddenly came round to it when they realised it was the only game in town. Well done, enlightened business leaders!

It is, however, vital that you remain the monarch of your domain, even if you are doing paid work in it. Any task that you don't want to perform, simply cite health and safety, council or building regulations or your tenancy agreement. After all, your employer can't tell you what you can and can't do in your own home.

'I'm afraid I'm unable to look at spreadsheets on Tuesdays, but that's what you get with a Labour council. I can look at amusing gifs all day, if you like. Well, not all day, but certainly ten to twelve.'

Employ a video background that suggests great discomfort, like the inside of a walk-in freezer, possibly with animal carcasses. Only a monster would want to extend a meeting in which you're suffering just to get the best signal. In no time at all you'll be back on the sofa, having a dhansak with Her Majesty.

DIY

Even the domestic idyll requires a certain level of maintenance which only indolence can temper.

Remember the tale of the three little pigs? The first little pig built his house out of straw. The second built his house out of wood. The third took ages building his house out of bricks and was very proud of himself. But when he got to the pub, he found the other two little pigs were already there, in the good seats. Makes you think, doesn't it?

The lazy are not natural DIY-ers, due to deficiencies in competence, focus, desire and a heartfelt belief that it is not what fingers were made for. The committed DIY-er, on the other hand, is naturally curious about how things work. He or she is a puzzle solver. On finding the printer not working, for example, their desire for knowledge will lead them to try to solve the mystery. We couldn't give a toss about the puzzle. We're more likely to chuck the puzzle in the bin and buy a new one that works and therefore is a printer again and not a puzzle. And even more likely than that to simply leave it where it is and do without a printer for evermore. Ruddy printers.

You may be inclined to blame the parents of these slackers, but, taking Dirty South as an example, it's not a theory that holds water. Dirty South's father was a fixaholic, whose weekends were filled with fixing not only his own stuff, but that of neighbours and acquaintances. (Though he drew the line at decorating: 'Whoever invented decorating wants fucking and whoever invented fucking wants decorating,' he would opine to a confused Little Dirty South.)

Old Dirty South was never happier than when mending things, or breaking them so he could fix them again. Unable to fathom that not everyone shared his enthusiasm, he'd cheerily ask his boy on a Saturday morning: 'Want a job, son?'

Head in hands, Dirty South would lament: *He simply has no idea who I am.* But, as we have already heard, he could hardly tell his dad that he was doing his homework. So the Dirty one would get dragged around by his dad as an assistant fixer, bewildered by the toolbox and at odds with the skills required to use anything from it. *When I'm old enough to own my own tools,* he said to himself, *I won't.*

The practical knowledge required for DIY tends to fall

to those most capable. It's not an accident. If, when a shelf falls down, your instinct is to turn off the football and reach for your tool bag, you've entered a mindset foreign to the Deserter. If you use the fallen shelf as an armchair tray for your rum and cashews, you're on the right track.

Obviously some malfunctions require action. If your car engine is making a terrible noise, you'll need to turn the music right up. Equally, if your toilet is blocked, there is nothing for it but to move home immediately.

Interestingly, noise is a key indicator as to whether or not a task should be attempted. The sound of a drill or angle grinder is alarming to everyone except the person making the racket. Everyone else thinks you're a dick for making such a row at that time of day, no matter what time of day it is. We use this rule of thumb: will this activity allow me to continue to ponder the mysteries of the universe, or at least watch *Bargain Hunt*?

Sadly, occasional repairs are necessary, but only once you've enquired, do I really need hot *and* cold running water when there's tapfuls of the stuff at Costa? Of course, if you can spare a few readies, you'll be inclined to get someone in who knows what they're doing. It will save you bringing down the national grid while trying to change a fuse and free you up for the things you excel at, like shove ha'penny and The Next One Who Comes Round The Corner, That's Who You're Going To Marry, That Is.

Dirty South did eventually stumble across a practical solution to the dilemma of how to fix things without fixing things. His missus. She does all the DIY and he does all the cooking in a comfortable and natural stereotype swap. Kind of like seahorses.

Housework

Sorry to break it to you, but there is no super-fun way to clean the home. No amount of party music and fetish wear can obscure the fact that it's a chore of the highest order. Unfortunately, chore or not, it needs to be done, like getting up in the night to take a leak, or destroying evidence. In a way, it is destroying evidence.

One cleaning tip that often crops up is to hold a cleaning party. The trouble with this proposition is that it requires friends who consider that a cleaning party is in any way tempting. It sounds a little like taking advantage of the mentally ill, or at the least, mildly OCD. Dirty South did once persuade Half-life to help him break the back of the grunge in his flat, telling him he'd just moved in and promising free food and booze. It worked up to a point, but then became a real party during which his place got trashed, the police were called and someone stole his front door. Curiously, Half-life's flat is spotless, but then he did win a cleaner in a poker game.

'Miss Maybe, she's called,' he says. 'A part-time burlesque dancer. Thing is, when she gets scrubbing I can't concentrate on *Countdown*.'

Another option, if you have a bit of outside space, is to start a bonfire. Poking at the flames with a big stick provides a primitive thrill that can be quite addictive, and before you know it, it's not just rubbish you're burning, it's tax forms, rickety furniture, resented pets and anything else that conspires to make the place untidy. Pro tip: in this instance it's legitimate to invite your friends round for a 'barbecue', only handing out the heavy-duty gloves on their arrival.

The Garden

If you have absolutely nothing else to do, gardening offers a chance to escape the rigours of the modern world and immerse yourself in nature, just as our forefathers once did. Indeed, do it for long enough and you'll begin to understand why our forefathers invented society in the first place.

Preparing the garden – the spadework – can be a back-breaking job and is usually enough to put off almost everyone. But gardening isn't just about constant bending and getting your hands dirty, or green, or whatever – there is also the offer of battery-charging quiet and solitude. The garden shed can be a wonderful place to call your own. There is little that some time alone with an old vice, a one-bar electric fire and some seedlings can't cure. Once you take in a mattress though, it's probably time to get a hold of yourself.

Planting flower beds and growing your own vegetables can provide a tremendous sense of accomplishment, even though you've largely just been standing around, leaning on a spade, honking on a hip flask. When deciding what to plant, consider your future requirements, including entertaining. We favour that most noble and versatile of vegetables, the potato. (They even have eyes. While lesser vegetables rot, potatoes *want to see*.) When you have guests over, who could fail to be delighted by some home-made cheesy chips or salt and vinegar crisps that have been *grown in your own garden*?

Being from the countryside, Roxy's approach to the urban garden is to fill the tiny space she's been allotted with various shades and sizes of flower and leaf, which gives her great pride and a sense of peace, even though it's all inedible and most of it unsmokeable. But what's this hidden behind the thick layer of jungle? A hot tub? With a fridge? You can take the girl out of the country, they say, but try getting her out of the Lay-Z-Spa Helsinki 2000 when she's on the cocktails.

'Keep your hobbies from becoming chores' goes the conventional wisdom, which is tricky with gardening since it's clearly both at the same time. Take mowing the lawn, for example. It's difficult to think of a better example of something that could wait until tomorrow. However, follow this simple procedure to simultaneously eliminate a chore and improve your downtime potential.

As spring approaches, explain to your other half how you've gone right off the 'bourgeois manicured look' in contemporary gardens and would prefer something a bit more 'expressive', a little more free. It's highly unlikely they'll even be listening, to be honest, but then when you next mow the lawn leave a far corner untouched and put a lounger in it. This should be known as your 'wilderness area'.

Talk about how happy and at peace it makes you. Then, each time you mow the lawn, ensure your wilderness area becomes a little bigger, until it stretches all the way to the kitchen door. *Et voilà*. No more lawn mowing and a place to call your own.

Now for that annual leave.

Shopping

Shopping for the home divides opinion. Dirty South finds the whole supermarket experience a soul-destroying invitation to overbuy, while the Dulwich Raider actively enjoys the hunt for bargains and the meditative benefits of driving a trolley.

The key is to make life easy for yourself. We advise having all heavy, bulky or dull goods – potatoes, toilet roll, laundry liquid (if required) – delivered on a repeat prescription. This leaves you free to swan about the more manageable shops with a baguette over your shoulder, a pocketful of parsley and a bottle of Cognac under your arm, like a French alcoholic.

Don't attempt too much shopping in one go. We like Dirty South's dictum on this: 'One bag: free; two bags: slave.' And never tell anyone you are going shopping – receiving texts like 'bin liners, dishwasher tablets' can ruin the mood of the casual shopper, especially when you're already down the caff.

Family

The bottom line is, if you want to dedicate your life to shirking, don't have a family. Children may be beautiful and inspire the most powerful love within you, but they don't half make it tricky to complete the Top Ten Pubs on a Roundabout Tour, certainly within the allotted time-frame. The little darlings play havoc with a life of naps and hangovers, not to mention your bank balance. However, children do happen. We don't know how, but they do. And there is very little information available on how to cope, beyond an entire arm of the publishing industry and something called the Internet.

Luckily, we're here to help. One thing the experts won't tell you is that your primary function as a parent is to render your little one unconscious as often and for as long as possible. This in itself should provide you with some time for life's pleasures. Unfortunately, you may find you are way too tired to take proper advantage of such opportunities. With this in mind, the location of your home is paramount. You need somewhere quiet, for example, and *no more than fifty metres from a pub.*

When flat-hunting, Dirty South always made a point of taking the baby monitor to viewings, which he would then carry to the local bar while the estate agent imitated a baby crying in the property in question. It certainly narrowed the field down – these locations are at a premium, and with good reason. When you're too tired to consider proper going out, popping over the road in your dressing gown 'to test the monitor's range' provides a disproportionate expansion of your horizon, beyond the babyworld bubble. Even if you've only got ten minutes, you can get one down and feel a little happier. Never mind the local school's Ofsted report. That could all change by the time the nipper is ready to attend. The baby monitor signal, however, will remain constant.

Some pubs actively encourage the pint and pushchair set with playrooms, adventure playgrounds and colouring books. Nonetheless, you will still need to bribe the bairn with all the things you won't let them eat at home if you want to have any hope of polishing off a bottle between you. Pro tip: always keep an eye on the weather if you're feeling stir crazy. At the first sign of storm clouds, pack the pushchair and head towards the park just before it starts to rain. Forced to escape the deluge in the pub, you are then trapped in licensed premises, but are simultaneously giving your partner a well-deserved break.

As we look beyond the baby and toddler stage we find balance is important in a happy family life. Previous generations tended to treat children as lovable inconveniences that should be seen and not heard. Parents would carry on with their lives and the kids would be dragged along with little consideration given to their interests: to the municipal dump, perhaps, a meeting of the Royal Philatelic Society, the outside of a pub. Hence the number of middle-aged people who fondly remember sitting in a locked car in a pub car park with a bag of crisps and a bottle of pop. There was no harm done, at least not until Dad got behind the wheel pished, but it's a practice that has slipped from the modern-day parenting manual.

Today, a remarkable transformation has occurred

whereby the children are a key part of the family decision-making process. Everything is geared not towards their needs, but their desires. Weekends are filled with things *they* want to do, that *you* have to accommodate, otherwise you may tear terrible fissures in their psyche that require expensive treatment in adulthood. They have developed the power of veto and get to choose where you go on holiday, what is viewed on TV and that you have to wear a Stormtrooper outfit for dress-down Friday.

As they get older and go out on their own, you are expected to remain sober *at the weekend* in order to pick them up, tipsy, possibly stoned and filled with rampant, ungrateful hormones that have rendered them unable to communicate except with grunts and emojis. On the plus side, you may be able to confiscate their stash from time to time, under the guise of good parenting.

The answer is to balance the two approaches. Don't ignore the little'uns' needs, but if you are going to be in charge of children, don't put them in charge. You must take care of your needs, too. Unhappy, put-upon parents are not good parents. Just as the air stewards tell you: put on your oxygen mask first, *then* that of your children. You must make sure you're OK, so you can make sure they're OK. There's no 'I' in 'team' and, equally, there's no 'U' in 'bad-tempered, unreasonable little shits'. Or only one, anyway.

GAMES TO PLAY WITH THE KIDS WHEN KNACKERED

Hospitals: Ideal for a rainy day with a raging hangover, you lie in bed moaning and hopefully napping, while being attended to by a child with a plastic stethoscope.

Lazy Deckchair Man: This popular garden game features a character (you) who very occasionally stirs to check that children have paid for their deckchairs. If they have not then they are given a count of 250 to run and hide, and then creep back to their chairs while you 'pretend' to sleep. Repeat.

Zipper Mouth: This is a simple, fun game to see who can keep quiet the longest. Not only can you get a moment's peace, you can also win.

Sleep Grand Prix: One for the more gullible child. You race them to sleep, in the hope, this time, that you lose.

Computer games: Bond with your offspring while lying on the sofa racking up record scores, teaching them hand-to-eye coordination and the value of leaping from platform to platform in the face of apparently unstoppable onslaughts by fire-gobbing flowers.

In conclusion, then, we broadly agree with the law that says you shouldn't, in all conscience, abandon your children, even if they are noisy, needy tinkers. However, you can maintain a reasonable level of loaf-time within the framework of having a family, and even, on occasion, find yourself able to achieve a glimpse of your pre-family life (see 'Leisure'). And maybe, if you're lucky, your children will grow up and one day drive you to the seaside and buy you lunch. Though we wouldn't count on it.

Coping with Christmas

God knows we're no theologians, but we understand that once Christmas had a religious significance and something to do with the concepts of fellowship, compassion and goodwill to all mankind. Now it's all about twatting each other in Tesco for a 50" TV, binge eating and piddling into a McFlurry cup on the last train home.

It is, nonetheless, a time when families gather in the home, to eat together, exchange gifts, express affection and hopefully get out before the tears and fighting. Properly planned, you can find moments to step outside the consumerist ordeal and domestic trauma and find a sort of seasonal peace. 'Preparation' is not a word you hear frequently in slacker salons, but a modicum of forethought can reap dividends for all. And in particular – and best of all – you.

Working

Most people already know that annual leave should not be taken pre-Christmas. There are simply too many free lunches, knock-off-earlies and drinks at your desk to be had. It's a ding dong merry malingerer's paradise.

Less obvious, perhaps, is the rule that you shouldn't take annual leave between Christmas and New Year. Not only do you get a break from the family, this period is ideal for the worker: the trains are empty, you can rock up at something past ten, sit alone in the office drinking tea, install a new OS on your phone, take a long lunch and piss off before four o'clock. Save your leave for proper working days, when people are trying to get things done.

Your holidays

During the Christmas break itself, remember at all times that you are on your holidays. In the run-up, be sure to let everyone know how much you need some time off.

'Sweet Jesus, this break can't come soon enough,' you might say, to anyone that will listen, but particularly to those with whom you will spend Christmas. 'My doctors have ordered complete rest. I'm a medical miracle. They're sending my notes to the World Health Organization.'

This sets the expectations of friends and family, making it clear that you cannot possibly be expected to do anything strenuous like clearing – or even standing – up over the holiday.

'Lovely to see you all!' you say, loudly, on arrival, as you flop onto the sofa, kick off your shoes, pull over the footstool and reach for the remote. 'My God, you don't know how much I've been looking forward to this.' And everyone will know not to bother you with something as trivial as the dishes.

Hiding

As a child, when you'd had enough of the family you could retreat to your room, peel a satsuma and stick on some Stockhausen. Now, for some reason, you're supposed to be 'around'.

When it comes to getting a little me time, it's no good

just standing in the larder with a pint of gin and tonic – lovely as that is, you'll be discovered in no time. Instead, make a big fuss about upgrading the WPA key on the router or sorting out that stuff for charity in the garage and you can buy yourself an hour with the radio here and there.

But nothing compares to the nap. If childcare is an issue, talk to your other half about 'tag-napping'. One of you sits with the kids, shelling walnuts in front of *Shaun the Sheep,* while the other lies face down on the bed for as long as it takes to feel human again, then you swap over. Let's face it, if you've been on the bubbles since breakfast, as you should be, you're going to need it.

Does your work mean that you have to be 'on call' over Christmas? If yes, excellent. If no, well it does now. Being on call serves multiple purposes. Firstly, it's vaguely impressive – someone, somewhere is relying on you, of all people. Secondly, it evokes sympathy in anyone you tell (which should be everyone). Inevitably, you will have to disappear for a couple of hours to sort that thing out with the guys in maintenance. But of course, you're not on call, you're driving around the empty streets, singing your tits off to Mariah Carey, just like last year.

Eating
There is a growing trend for eating out on Christmas Day. We would counsel against this. Eating Christmas

lunch out is expensive, loud, busy and tiring – everything we stand against. Sure, you may save on the washing-up but, as we've already established, you're in no shape to do the washing-up anyway, you're too drunk and ill. No, there's nothing for it but to hit the aforementioned bubbles early and sail through to lunch, after which you can crash on the sofa and miss the entire film that everyone was looking forward to, including you.

Post-Christmas

The days between Christmas and New Year – the perineum of the year – would, on the face of it, seem like the ideal time to do your tax return or replace all the dead light bulbs in the house. A kind of peace has fallen upon the house. But desist. Ask yourself, what's wrong with going out? Gone are the party hats, the queues and the basins filled with sick. You've got your lovely pub back. At least for a few days, until the amateurs all come out again for New Year's Eve.

Dhansak with Her Majesty
Tapfuls of the stuff at Costa
No to the bourgeois manicured look
One bag: free; two bags: slave
Live no more than fifty metres from a pub
My doctors have ordered complete rest

MONEY

'I have enough money to last me the rest of my life,
unless I buy something.'

– Jackie Mason, comedian

♦ How to Get It ♦ Retire Early
♦ Live Like a King on Nearly Nowt

It doesn't grow on trees, it can't buy you love and it makes the world go round. What are we talking about? No, not the rotational inertia of accreted matter, but money.

Economists define money as something that serves as a medium of exchange. It's what you have to hand over to get a new phone or that fortnight in Ibiza. But the greatest thing that money can buy, or should buy, is freedom. Freedom from financial worries, freedom from bosses, freedom from jobs you loathe.

Money offers a glimpse of the only goal worth concerning yourself with: freedom of choice. On being asked, 'Is that with beans or cheese?' when ordering the Baked Potato Meal Deal No. 3, for example, there is no better feeling than responding with a wave of the hand and a carefree, 'Both!'

'You do know that will be an extra £1.20,' may come the reply. But you can just nod and smile your sad smile. And they will know that you are truly free.

Chasing wealth purely for wealth's sake is to be avoided. It can play havoc with your health and your time, not to mention your soul. It simply costs too much. On the other hand, a lack of money can condemn you to a life of drudgery, as you grind out an existence simply to be able to afford a sofa to rest on after work. Or worse, debt and poverty.

One reasonable rule of thumb is that we require just as much money as it takes to allay our fears of destitution, and no more. The key here is balance. It's an inconvenient truth that we all need cash. But we must learn to master it, or it will master us.

How to Get It

Inheritance

The simplest way to get money is to inherit it, which is why the upper classes love it so. There's no work involved, no test of your talent and you don't even have to get out of your four-poster waterbed to earn it. However, there is nothing you can do to influence the wealth of those who have gone before you. The best you can do is look to the future and identify any distant relative who might have a few bob and send them a Chocolate Orange once in a while. Remember to include a picture of children with the gift – they don't have to be yours.

Roxy's Auntie Dave has added her to her will in return

for Roxy taking her out once a month and showing her a right rollicking good time. 'She's great company, drinks like a fish and pays for everything,' she tells us. 'Unfortunately she also loves going to Andrew Lloyd Webber shows, so, ironically, I may have to kill her.'

If you're not fortunate enough to come into money, however, all may not be lost. The Raider had an interesting experience when, aged nineteen, his father took him to one side and gravely informed him that not only had Mad Uncle Cyril sadly passed away, but that he had given away the entire and substantial family fortune to a French prostitute named Fifi.

'It all made complete sense, my innate sense of wealth,' he recalls. 'I'd always swanned about like landed gentry, just without the land. Or the swans.'

He claims his immediate reaction was to take the unusual step of putting himself up for adoption, in the hope of finding some parents with some lolly in the bank. Or at least a nice car. When they refused to countenance this he sued them for incompetence and being drunk in charge of a relative.

'In the end I settled out of court for a new bike and a dartboard. Result. Later in life, oddly, I came to consider Mad Uncle Cyril something of a hero and now also look forward to moving to the Côte D'Azur in my twilight years.'

Gambling

Gambling is not for everyone. Fortunately, it is best suited to sports nuts who like making money, tax-free, while watching TV in their smalls.

Although it may sound strange, gambling should not be left to luck and certain rules should be adhered to, to optimise your chance of making money. For example, only bet on sports you know and understand, with a set amount you can afford to lose, say, each month. Homework is important here, but fortunately this is just reading and talking about sports, so doesn't feel like real work at all.

Use your knowledge of a sport to bet, preferably 'in-play', which will allow you to respond to in-game trigger points and cut your losses (or take your profits early) using a 'cash-out' facility should events conspire against you. Do not be concerned about or put off by losing bets; this system is about regular gambling to make a small profit each month and losing here and there is inevitable.

'Not gambling because you lost is like not asking out any more girls because you got knocked back once,' says Dirty South, probably thinking about the time Rachel Stevens laughed at his moustache.

When you have increased your original stake by a certain previously agreed (with yourself) amount, withdraw your profit. For example, you might allow yourself an initial float of £50. And each time you reach £100, withdraw your profits, leaving your initial £50 with which to go again. Importantly, if you lose your initial float, then you must wait again until next month. That is your punishment for failure.

What we're saying, essentially, is that there is – or should be – a skill to gambling, one that requires dedication and a clear head. Sadly this means that, as with driving or needlework, drink and drugs should be strictly off limits while you engage in it, which is a shame because, like driving (though unlike needlework), it is tremendous fun to do when tipsy. There are some bets, however, that guarantee a return (see Live Like a King on Nearly Nowt, below), leaving you able to get wrecked on your winnings before you've even won, like some sort of hedge fund time traveller.

It's also worth noting Roxy's pioneering work in the area of what she terms 'Compensation Betting'. A keen Reading FC fan, due to being brought up in somewhere called 'Berks', she will ask herself each weekend what it is worth to her for the Royals to win. Sometimes the answer is a tenner; sometimes, if she's feeling flush or it's a grudge game, it's £50.

She then takes that money and *bets that Reading will not win*. The idea being that if they do win, she is happy, and if they do not, then at least she has made some wedge to help her get over it. In recent seasons, it has to be said, this has become quite a rich source of income for her. Roxy reports that her boyfriend even took to checking to see if Reading had lost to see if they'd be eating out that evening.

Investing

Investing is gambling too, but for some reason it has a different name. However, you are statistically more likely to reap some reward – or, at least, not lose all your money. Instead of playing the lottery or buying premium bonds (both essentially a tax on those with a poor grasp of mathematical probability) we suggest finding a low-cost equity broker and buying shares in companies that you like, that you see being run well or that, as a share-holder, you would like to influence.

When the Dulwich Raider, for example, realised that he was using online takeaway service Just Eat twice a week, he bought shares in the company. A year later he had doubled his money. Now he uses it four nights a week.

The touchstones here are:

• Invest in stocks and shares within an ISA and, as with gambling, all your profits will be tax-free, delivering all the benefits of tax avoidance without the stigma of getting involved in offshore film funding schemes that never fund any films. Or worse, finance Guy Ritchie.

- Avoid investing with the herd. If everyone's rushing to invest it's likely to be a bubble, and bubbles pop. As John D. Rockefeller noted, it's time to get out of the stock market when the bellhop in your hotel starts giving you share tips.

- Again, only invest what you can afford to lose (or at least tie up for a good while) and never borrow to invest, unless you work in a bank, when that is your actual job.

- Don't get greedy. Keep in the mind the attitude of legendary Wall Street investor Bernard Baruch. When friends ribbed him about selling out of companies too early he responded, 'Yes, I made all my money selling too soon.'

Bank robbery

'Give me one good reason why not,' said Half-life, when we chuckled at his contribution to this section. And perhaps he has a point.

Robbing a bank is not a victimless act, but as the victims are corrupt, soulless, offshore merchants of exploitation and misery, it is certainly worth considering. Furthermore, as we now know, any losses incurred by banks are made good from the public purse.

You will, however, need to consult your own legal advisers on this, as in many countries theft remains illegal.

Dole

'I don't know how I would have got through the nineties without it,' recalls Half-life. 'You didn't have to jump through all the fucking hoops you have to now. You just showed up every fortnight, they sent you a cheque, you bought your weed. Job done. Or rather, no job done. And you got your rent paid. It was a simpler time. More romantic.'

Indeed, the two weeks between signing-on days allowed for a succession of European jaunts.

'I drove to Czechoslovakia in a camper van after signing on, once,' says the big man. 'Was supposed to be going to Spain to get away from the winter but we took a wrong turn at Paris. Ten below zero and a van full of cheesecloth and espadrilles. But my God we lived like kings. One pound got you a box at the opera, a bottle of Russian Champagne and ten packs of fags. But the van was fucking freezing so we moved into the top floor of the best hotel in Plzeň. Too good to leave, so I got Strange Martin to sign on for me in return for a pair of skis. Though I lost one of them on the Autobahn.'

Now known as Jobseeker's Allowance, the process for receiving this unemployment assistance grows ever more arcane. There are two types, contributory and income-related, the latter being means tested and replaced by Universal Credit. You can apply for it if you are working fewer than sixteen hours a week but only if your partner is working fewer than twenty-four hours a week. You must be able to work, be actively seeking employment, be able to prove this on demand and promise not to drive to Prague.

Is it any wonder that all but the most desperate and needy in our society have turned their backs on this once-glorious state benefit?

'What are you on about?' says Half-life. 'I'm still on it.'

Universal Basic Income

Having learned how tiresome money can be to acquire, we come to one of the cornerstones of our economic model: the advocacy of a universal basic payment for everyone in the universe. It goes something like this: no matter what your circumstances, once you reach the age of eighteen you will be paid £800 a month to do with what you will, and regardless of whether you choose to work for income on top of that.

It's not a new idea: Sir Thomas More suggested it in *Utopia* (1513), for the simple reason that 'no one should die of hunger'. Clearly modern society knows better.

Trials in Iran a decade ago found that the recipients did not remove themselves from the labour market, as had been feared. Only those in their twenties actually did less work, which suggests we should listen to the wisdom of the young. A subsequent pilot scheme in Finland found participants were 'happier but jobless', according to a BBC News headline that spectacularly missed the point. Compared to the control group, it made little or no difference to their finding jobs, but they had better mental health and were more fun to be around.

UBI would, simply put, eradicate poverty. That is hugely significant and surely a key duty of any government. It would allow workers to reject low wages, fund unpaid carers, let victims of domestic violence get the hell out and allow people to find out what they really want to do with their lives and support them doing it. In short, it would help people be happier. Sure, some people might lie around all day, eating cherries and masturbating. We say, crucially, let them. Not in public, though, to be fair. Enough is enough.

How would it be paid for? By dismantling a redundant means-tested benefits system and legalising (and taxing) drugs, for a start. At a stroke, wealth would be redistributed to those who don't have it, rather than waiting for it to somehow magically 'trickle down' to the poorest in society, like monetary Golden Syrup. Trickle-down economics is a fallacy. The rich don't want anything to trickle down, not their syrup and particularly not their money.

For too long the focus has been on job creation and employment figures as the signs of a healthy economy. We urge governments everywhere to heed our cry: we don't want the jobs, we just want the money.

Work

Sorry. But in a section on how to get money, there it is.

If you have to work – and it's a sad indictment of our so-called society that most of us will have to at some point – then at least try to gravitate, however infinitesimally, towards something you actually like doing, or that you believe in, or is simply piss-easy. Given that you will be handing over the best years of your life to an employer, gift-wrapped in your own skin, it really can help in the long run.

Failing that, at least get a seat near someone good-looking.

THE GAME (ADVANCED MODULE)

Corporate insider Ivan Osman refers to work as 'The Game'. For him, work is an elaborate delayed gratification exercise in which, to put it bluntly, you sentence yourself to fifteen years or so of hard labour in a well-paid industry in order to eventually win back your liberty; to buy yourself out.

During this period you are required to look after yourself, to rise early, to focus, fawn, study, listen, adapt and, worst of all, be bored – all the things you swore you'd never put up with. Your aim: to rise as high as possible up the corporate ladder. Friends may accuse you of 'selling out', but Osman counters this with a wry smile, saying, 'You're right, of course. To be honest, if it wasn't for all the drugs, money and sex, I'd be out of there like a shot.' And they fall silent.

At the end of The Game, you emerge chastened but mortgage-free and ready to party for your remaining years, juggling the odd four-days-per-annum executive directorship with, for example, actual juggling. This, we stress, is a long-term gambit for the advanced student, for which a steely resolve and a strong sense of self is a minimum requirement, lest you get sucked into the system, distracted by the gilt on the inside of your cage and lose sight of the ultimate prize: freedom.

Retire Early

The simple goal of the Deserter is to find more time for messing around before it's too late. It's worth remembering, after all, that you are currently the youngest you will ever be. To this end we suggest retiring immediately. If this is impractical, at least look into winding down your working days.

Financially, we recommend working backwards from what you actually require in order to have a life worth living. If you can live happily on £1,000 a month, then earn £12k and take the rest of the year off. If you find you need three grand a month, then £36k per annum is your goal and it's possible some sort of a career will be required. If you require twenty grand a month then, really, have a word with yourself.

By all means earn more than you need, but if your

spending increases accordingly you are only stealing time from your future self. Imagine old you discovering that you still have to get up and go to work for years due to young you splashing Bolly all over your new shoes in the back of a cab home from Claridge's on a Tuesday. Any extra money should be stashed or invested (see above) so as to foreshorten your working existence and fast-forward to the good life.

The trick here is not to get overfamiliar with luxury. Too much luxury ceases to be luxury and becomes the new normal, and surely you must be worth normal, right? Beware. The moment you catch yourself taking a swish hotel room for granted, for example, it's time to down-grade to a night in a tent on a static caravan park to teach yourself a lesson. For us, a life of frugal but determined pleasure-seeking is vastly preferable to one spent in emotional or financial chains, despite the odd perk here and there.

Furthermore, a recent German study on retirement overturned the accepted wisdom that people keel over and die a fortnight after being given the golden pocket watch. In fact, retired people turned out to be healthier and happier than when they were working: sleeping better, visiting their doctors less and generally having it large. The lesson? Do not leave retirement to the old: the money's rubbish, but the hours are great.

When Spider returned from his African adventure with the Dobe !Kung, he was a changed man, and not just because he was now sporting a ponytail and a long beard. Back in London, he was put in mind of Conrad's Marlow, returned from the Congo in *Heart of Darkness*: 'I found myself back in the sepulchral city resenting the sight of people hurrying through the streets to filch a little money from each other . . . to dream their insignificant and silly dreams.' In his native Manchester, where he was renamed Fiasco da Gama (by his mother), he felt further confined by conformity and prejudice.

It was a difficult time for him. 'I bet you're all wearing underwear, aren't you?' he exclaimed to us one afternoon on the South Bank, before throwing his shoes in the river and wandering off, barefoot.

Unwilling and unable to return to a life of work, he was alarmed to discover that there were now an additional ten hours a day available for smoking, drinking and binge eating, not to mention that he could holiday whenever he pleased. Within a year he had spent all his savings, and a bit more. Luckily for him, he had bought a smart two-bedroom house in south-east London which, with the help of a broker he met in his local, he was able to remortgage and top up the coffers.

With his bank account back in the black, he packed his bags and rented out the house. If he lived carefully, he reasoned, in places where his money went a little further, here was a chance to set himself loose upon the world, a free man. He could travel, he could learn, he could steep himself in new ways, new cultures. Although, in reality, his travels mainly seemed to coincide with the tours of the England cricket team.

An example to us all, though most of us will not be so fortunate.

Live Like a King on Nearly Nowt

The key to both an early retirement and a happy retirement is to live within your means and not to blow what little money you have cobbled together over your lifetime. This doesn't mean you shouldn't live well – or as well as possible – it just means you may have to learn some new tricks.

Once you've got your hands on some moolah, for God's sake don't start throwing it around like you're one of the super-rich. You're not one of the super-rich, you're you, and very likely all the better for it. If you've ever encountered the rude misery guts that frequent first-class flight cabins or five-star hotels you will know what we mean.

Next time you consider upgrading to a new car or splashing out on a drone to follow you around with a box of doughnuts, consider this: you are not paying for it with money, you are paying for it with your time – the time it took you to earn that money.

Picasso said, 'I'd like to live as a poor man with lots of money,' which sounds to us like a reasonable dictum, as long as he chipped in for lunch. If you can make your money last, you're one step closer to working less and doing more of what you want to do.

For the skiver, sneaking out of the office for a fry-up, fabricating an all-day 'conference' in a seaside town or leaving work at 4 p.m. to see a periodontist who just happens to be practising near a riverside pub is not enough. A taste of such delights merely leaves an appetite for more and before you know it you're doing a Dirty South and emailing your boss about going down to three days a week, then two, and so on until there are no more days left to reduce. This will naturally lead to a drop in income but, cruelly, more time in which to spend it. You have been caught in Spider's Web.

The temptation initially may be to stay in bed, and many people do spend their early days of freedom under the duvet. But ultimately the Deserter is driven to seek new and exquisite pleasures in ever more unlikely places; to use their time wisely, even when boracic.

Contrary to expectations perhaps, when not working we're up and raring to go each morning. Around eleven. And while there is plenty to enjoy for nowt, some things just cost money. Not our rules, the rules of post-industrial capitalist society. So, in an effort to solve the time-rich/ cash-poor conundrum, in this section we offer some suggestions on ways to supplement your income and/or make a little go a long way.

In short, how to live like a king on nearly nowt.

Mystery shopping

Shopping may be a mystery to many of us, but this is shopping with a twist for those that are a) skint and b) fussy buggers who like nothing better than to bang on about standards of cleanliness, service, food or beverages.

As a mystery shopper you turn up to places incognito with a brief to eat lunch or get a haircut, fill out a form about your experience and then get paid a fee (plus expenses). On offer are visits to leisure centres, hotels, bars, restaurants and, our favourite, the bookies, where you get paid to place free bets and have a go on the machines.

In the interests of research Dulwich Raider signed up and treated Dirty South to lunch, gratis. They feasted, got drunk, befriended their waitress and awarded her the optional £50 bonus voucher for exceptional performance, which she generously shared in the form of house rosé. A top afternoon, what they can remember of it.

The downsides are that the forms are laborious and the payments are small. You're not going to make a living being mysterious in shops, but you will get a wide selection of freebies.

Search 'Market Force', 'Storecheckers' or 'Grass Roots Mystery Shopping'.

Parking

'There's a strange car in our drive,' said the Raider to his wife recently.

'I know,' she replied. 'I'm letting it out. A tenner a day.'

'Wow. What are we going to do with the money?' he asked

'I thought we could hire a gardener,' she said.

'Oh, right,' said the Raider.

'Only kidding, let's go for lunch,' she said, which goes a long way to explain why he married her.

Note: you do not actually need to own your own house to sign up, you just need a drive. Or, if you're feeling cheeky, someone else's.

Search 'JustPark' or 'Park On My Drive'.

Freecycle

Pick up someone's unwanted clobber via Freecycle and not only are you helping to prevent landfill, you're doing them a favour. The danger is that you're also cluttering up your place with desks, bicycles, washing machines and drum kits you don't need, let alone want. The sad truth is, Swingball's shit in the kitchen.

However, ever since Roxy picked up Otto, her silver Toyota Corolla, on Freecycle we admit to firing up the listings from time to time to have a nose through what's being offered, despite the bag of liver she found in the glove compartment.

Search 'Freecycle'. Gumtree and Craigslist also list freebies.

Matched betting

Betting companies frequently offer free bets in an attempt to encourage new customers. Used judiciously, these can guarantee returns, which you are free to withdraw as soon as your account has been credited. For example, you can use a free bet to bet on a particular sporting outcome (e.g. a home win) and then, using a betting exchange, place another free bet on the opposite occurring (in this case, that there will not be a home win).

Now, you're a winner either way and you can order a pizza for half-time. You've earned it, kind of.

Search 'Matched Betting'.

Cheap eats

It's always worth checking the supermarkets for reduced items towards the end of the day. Visit the discounted section and you can pick up a selection of fine food that has to be eaten that evening. In the interests of research we tried this for a week but after a nightly diet of venison, pheasant and salmon *en croûte* we found ourselves yearning for the simple pleasure of a buttered baked potato and a tin of beans. Proof that the best things aren't always the most expensive.

To eat out on a budget, get a Tastecard. For a small fee you get 50 per cent off or '2 for 1' in more than 7,000 restaurants. It's a no-brainer, and they're not even giving us anything to say that, the tightwads.

Yes, the restaurant choice is limited, and, yes, it includes a lot of chains, but you can usually find something decent when the urge takes you and the card will have paid for itself within a couple of meals. As Half-life puts it, 'Anyone who pays full price at Pizza Express is a cunt.' Though even he conceded this was unlikely to get past the top brass at Tastecard as a marketing slogan.

Or you could take a leaf out of Dirty South's Book of Charm and add a veneer of romance to your money-saving meals. During the numerous lockdowns in the time of Covid-19, the Dirty one spotted his partner's mood plummeting. They hadn't been out in months and, with everything closed, there was little prospect of changing the dynamic of their life, which consisted of home schooling and completing Netflix.

So, setting off in advance, he asked her to meet him at a closed pub where they could still sit outside and enjoy a view. There, he produced a bottle of wine and a bag of chips from his bag and lit some candles. For under a tenner they had a candlelit meal for two, looking out over some greenery. They broke the cycle of monotony and had a giggle. She decided to keep him, despite his being the laziest man on Earth – and a cheapskate to boot.

Bargain booze

We were recently invited out for the evening by some young folk, who, showing a wisdom beyond their years, planned to spend it in a car park near an off-licence.

We're all for this as a reliably cheap form of entertainment, but of course it can be jazzed up a little.

One of our favourite gambits is to BYOB to grand public buildings: art galleries, theatres, monasteries. Once there, raid the water jug area for some plastic cups (and ice, if you're lucky), grab a table and drink in the edifying views – as well as the screw-top wine you brought with you. These places aren't like pubs, where such a practice will be frowned upon. They are public spaces, and as such are ideal for us to express our appreciation through the medium of alcohol. Indeed, the Dulwich Raider held his wedding reception in the grand courtyard of Somerset House, a stunning neoclassical building that is open to the public. Cost of landmark riverside venue hire in central London: £0.

In the summer months, as we have noted previously, parks offer a charming respite from the hurly burly, particularly in the company of a mate and a six-pack. In addition, for now at least, you can light up a doobie to optimise your latent love of nature.

Parks have been a feature of British life for centuries, but, as noted previously, they really came into their own during the pandemic. With pubs closed, they were the places friends could gather, share a toast and talk utter nonsense again. A lifesaver. And, once you clock that no one is ever going to bring you a bill, these new habits will die hard. Park-pubbing is here to stay.

Happy hours provide great succour for the impoverished drinker, but we generally favour permanent discounts. Wetherspoon pubs divide opinion, but with pints starting at £2 (less if you're a member of CAMRA) they basically allow you to have the student experience of half-price drinking. Or you could always become a student.

Become a student

Remember those years lounging around, sitting in each other's laps, reading paperbacks, snorting plant food and avoiding the rugby club? No, nor do we, but with e-Careers you get a chance to put that right by becoming a student again.

Sign up for any e-Careers online course and you are eligible for an NUS card (now known as TOTUM). The Dulwich Raider discovered this when he enrolled on a course in the dark arts of Google Analytics. It cost him just £19.99 (via Groupon) but in fact there are even cheaper courses. The cheapest we could see was one in accounting and bookkeeping for £9, though you may, understandably, consider that a bridge too far.

Armed with your NUS/TOTUM card (just enter 'e-Careers' when you're asked for your 'institution') you can then take on the world from a position of economic might. The vast range of benefits includes discounts on eating out, technology, clothes and food, plus concessionary rates for gigs and sporting events. *Finally*, the Raider's education pays off.

Search 'e-Careers' on Groupon or Wowcher.

Choose rich friends

If you happen to be a real student, or are about to become one, take the opportunity in this new phase in your life to acquire some wealthy friends.

These will usually be the ones riding e-scooters or propping doors open with polo mallets, but there is no need to leave this to chance. Simply obtain the addresses of as many people as possible in your year (perhaps under the pretence of sending them a small gift) and spend some time looking them up on Google Street View. If any of their addresses have a sign outside that reads 'These grounds are not open to the public', hey presto, you have found your new BFF and you'll be able to enjoy free ski-breaks and Mediterranean sailing trips for many years to come.

Some may baulk at such a brazen attempt at insinuating yourself into the circles of the wealthy elite, but, remember, it's not the principle, it's the money.

Back in the real world, generous friends are a boon in hard times. If you have cash, be generous – one day it may be you in need. Shout out to Roxy on this one.

'I'm not gonna lie, you guys are better after a few,' she says, as she starts up another bar tab on her business account. 'So it's in my interest to keep you well oiled.' What a woman. What a friend.

Finally, we sought the counsel of some of the crew for extra tips on living the good life on a budget:

Roxy: 'Vape pure grass in a loose-leaf cartridge for the v2 Pro Series 3X and you'll save a fortune on tobacco,' suggested Roxy. We're not entirely sure what she's on about but, by Christ, the last time we saw her she was having the time of her life.

Dulwich Raider: 'Catching sight of Mrs Raider on *Holby City* recently reminded me that not only had I forgotten to bring in the washing, but also that being a TV and movie extra is a good source of additional income. The work can be very sporadic and shouldn't be relied upon to pay the rent, but it does offer the chance to earn decent money for what is basically hanging around. The catering is excellent and there's always the chance of standing next to Sienna Miller in the queue for the Portaloo. Mrs Raider's top tip: if they ask whether you can bring a dog, say yes even if you have to borrow one. Those with pets always get let out early and you can be back in bed by 2 p.m.'

Dirty South: 'Crisp sandwiches,' said the Dirty one, without missing a beat. 'All the goodness of roast beef and mustard, with added potato, bread and butter.'

Half-life: 'That's easy,' said Half-life, leaning across the bar and topping up his pint. 'If they don't want you to help yourself, how come I can reach the taps?'

In conclusion, we urge that you do not obsess over money or worry about not being rich. If being rich is so great, how come so many rich people continue to devote themselves to becoming richer, instead of nicer? What is the point of wealth if it does not free you of the need to accrue ever more wealth? We return to our earlier point: how much money do you actually need? And when are you going to enjoy what you have?

Beans *and* cheese
Sell too early
Theft remains illegal
Get a seat near someone good-looking
We don't want the jobs, we just want the money.
Swingball's shit in the kitchen
Reach for the taps

HEALTH & BEAUTY

'If you give up fags, booze and fucking, you don't
actually live longer; it just seems like it.'

– Auntie Dave, bon viveur

♦ The Pitfalls of Pleasure ♦ Diet and Dieting
♦ Exercise ♦ Spa Break ♦ Grooming ♦ Relieve Stress . . .
♦ . . . Build Confidence

What does healthy living and looking after yourself have to do with anything?, you might ask, perhaps while dancing on a table with your trousers on your head. *Is it not at odds with the unfettered pursuit of fun advocated elsewhere in these pages?*

If you'd just come down for a moment, we'll explain. It's no good going around trying to maximise pleasure when you're in no fit state to enjoy it. Pleasure is the domain of the healthy – something you tend to forget until you're laid up with a bad back or are the innocent victim of a messy all-nighter.

A little self-care allows you to indulge in things that are less healthy (and more fun). Doctors advise taking a couple of consecutive days off the sauce each week, for instance. Abstaining on a Monday and Tuesday not only imbues Wednesday with scintillating purpose (and ensures your first tipple will be accompanied by a heavenly choir), but you are also likely to have more weeks in which to enjoy your favourite vices.

Our bodies are machines for living, and a little maintenance along the way can prevent the need for wholesale repairs further down the line. Think of your body as a car: a service here and an MOT there (actually a legal requirement, whatever Half-life says) can help keep you off the scrapheap.

OK, you can get back on the table now.

With something as life-affirming as Deserting, there are bound to be some liabilities on the balance sheet (if you ever got round to making one). You are taking steps to work less, worry less and get more fun into your life. But before we go on to discuss the costs of living well, let us not forget the perils of working your arse off for fifty years. Depression, often brought on by the terrible knowledge that your life's work is a meaningless barter in which you give your best years in exchange for permission to live, is a waking nightmare. Then there's the lack of sleep, which can lead to heart disease, diabetes and, worse, bags under your eyes. And finally, stress: insidious worry, gnawing away at your health and character, making you irritable, anxious, prone to illness and terrible company at parties.

According to the World Health Organization, hundreds of thousands of people die from overwork every year. This is not the glorious death of soldiers defending their homeland, but the misguided protection of someone else's priorities. CEOs who don't know you exist; business owners who fancy sipping champers in space.

So unless you're doing work you love, that makes you happy, you are not only exchanging your time, you could also be gambling with your health. You owe it to yourself to be free of the yoke of overwork. Just be careful you don't, in the process of reinventing yourself as a pure pleasure seeker, go too far the other way . . .

The Pitfalls of Pleasure

Obesity

There are risks of weight gain on the hedonist's horizon, largely because he or she is always available for treats under the merest provocation. Nobody said it would be easy. Not only are we ever ready to spring into action for a lunchtime snifter, the subsequent lost afternoon can give rise to a fearful hangover and a redemptive full English in the morning. That adds up to a lot of calories, which over the years can lead to a less than athletic frame.

However, it needn't be this way. We need more than booze alone. Sitting in a bar all day, every day, is not emancipation, it's alcoholism. That is why God put distances between pubs, so you could get a good constitutional walk in between and give your liver a break (pub crawls should not actually be done on all fours, remember). Fresh air, exercise, contemplation, the bookies . . . It's all there for you. Drinking eight pints is not an achievement. Enjoying them in half a dozen different locations, covering miles as you wander in company that makes you laugh and even think . . . now that is heroic.

A little timber on the bones is nothing to worry about, but obesity reduces life expectancy, and if there's anything the Deserter enjoys, it's life. The next body mass classification down from obese is 'pre-obese', and it is to this grand title that we recommend one aspires to. If necessary, say it out loud to yourself, or write it on your bathroom mirror: 'I *will* be pre-obese.'

Going to the gym, jogging and yoga seem such joyless pursuits, though we accept that the only way to find this out for sure is to try them. We concede that exercise does release endorphins (chemicals produced naturally by the body that boost happiness and relieve pain), making you actually want more of the stuff. And it certainly gives that first pint a well-earned feeling, as you sit there in your singlet, high as a kite. So whatever effort you are comfortable making in this department, hats off. Just remember not to talk, blog or post about it.

Drug addiction

Reality, like growing up, is overrated. It's no wonder we find ways to avoid it. However, reality is a necessary ground point to have, otherwise how do you know when you're high? And if you can't appreciate being in a rare, special place, then it ceases to be special.

When you come round at four in morning, in the lavs, perhaps, of the twenty-four-hour McDonald's (sorry, Roxy), it's time to call it a day. At least until next weekend. If we reach for another drink or a line or a pill at that point then we have clearly lost control. And we need to be in control of the medicine, otherwise our free will has been surrendered, rather than exercised. Drug addiction is boring, no matter what your poison. Addicts have forgotten that pleasure is enhanced by being uncommon. The urge for temporary fun is replaced with the need to maintain equilibrium, like working to pay off your overdraft. Beware.

Having said that, here's an at-a-glance guide to good gear, put together by our drugs tsar, Half-life.

Drug	Effect
Weed	'Giggles and great philosophical certainty about something you can't quite remember.'
Ket	'Good for wading through rugs and climbing into paintings.'

Coke	'How does it feel to turn down a line of cocaine? No one knows. Turns a normal person into a wanker and a wanker into a cunt. And I'm already a cunt, so that's alright.'
MDMA/ Ecstasy	'Makes you skip down streets and feel up lamp posts.'
Shrooms	'Can turn a Londis into a fabulous crystal castle of dreams.'
Acid	'I said, "Gran, have you seen my pills? They're marked 'LSD'." 'She goes, "Never mind the pills, there's a fucking unicorn in the kitchen."'
Opiates	'Need strong character and a will of iron for these, so not for the likes of you losers.'

Yes, opiates present a danger. Remaining in control of something so powerful may not be possible. That's why we're saving them for our dotage, when bits are starting to fall off. Heroin is a central plank in the plan for our final years and will ensure we don't suffer the slow descent into death of previous generations. When we can no longer enjoy a chat, or music, or travel, we'll still be able to take that holiday in our own minds. At that point, who cares about addiction? The only potential issue is, how do you score smack in your eighties? Best stockpile now, or become a pharmacist.

All intoxicants make good lovers, but poor masters, so

you need a firm hand on the tiller. Substance addiction poses the same risk as alcoholism, but happy, balanced people rarely fall into the trap of letting drugs do the thinking for them. Having more time on your hands is only really a health risk if you have pre-existing issues. It is therefore less likely, in our view, to turn you into an addict than going to work in a job you hate.

Gout

It's not often you get compliments with a medical diagnosis.

'Ah, the disease of kings,' smiled the benign doctor after Dirty South told her his symptoms. It felt, he said, like his foot was being stomped on by an invisible woman in stilettos.

'A beautiful, invisible woman in stilettos,' he told her.

Gout isn't an awful lot of fun, but at least you have to have an awful lot of fun to get it in the first place. There is no such thing as free gout. You really do have to put your hours in.

'Gout and proud!' tweeted the Dirty one, as he left the surgery.

It is, though, rather painful, particularly if someone steps on your toe. If you wear an appropriate badge, you should be able to get a seat on the bus – or indeed, back at the bar. Dietary causes for gout include overindulgence in such things as alcohol, meat, fructose-sweetened drinks and herring. It almost goes without saying that if yours isn't caused by alcohol and meat you need to take a long hard look at your choices.

Gout is treatable, in the first instance with NSAIDs (nonsteroidal anti-inflammatory drugs) and with other clever stuff if it persists. It is inconvenient when it first strikes, but, as we have seen, it is nothing compared to the horrors visited upon those who are working too hard – the diseases of the ill-advised.

If you do get gout, at least you're in good company. Famous gout sufferers include actor Jared Leto, though he did get it while putting on sixty pounds to play a role as a fat psycho. OK, not a great example.

'Aussie footballer Harry Kewell had a gout attack that kept him out of a World Cup game,' reports Dirty South. 'Makes me feel better about my lack of sporting achievement, as I too was kept out of international football, albeit for different reasons.'

Isaac Newton, Samuel Johnson, Nostradamus and Karl Marx all had gout too, so don't feel bad about it. It's a disease that reflects the care you've taken to enjoy your life. And then there's Henry VIII, who probably gave rise to it being called the disease of kings. It's true he was a cantankerous egotist with a callous disregard for human life, who advanced his personal desires under the guise of morality. Nobody's perfect. But he was also a visionary leader, a learned man, an accomplished musician, a poet, author and sportsman, who liked grog and gambling. What's not to like? Oh, yes. The callous disregard for human life.

Diet and Dieting

There is no doubt that many diets can lead to weight reduction. What happens then is that you come off the diet, put the weight back on, then go on another diet. Now it's Diet Industry 2, You 0 and it's not even half-time. Plus, you're constantly anxious over your body shape when you should be worrying about how you can fit going to work into a week packed with daydreams.

It cannot be a coincidence that the word 'Weight-watchers' contains the word 'twat'. It's a clue that right-thinking people do not diet; they permanently modify their lifestyle.

The Dulwich Raider tried the 5:2 diet for a while, on which you (almost) fast for two days a week. He liked it because whenever he felt hungry he could say to himself (usually out loud), 'I shall have chips tomorrow!', which he found very helpful. He did lose some weight on it but by month four he was worn out and contracted shingles (and, ironically, lost another stone). The 5:2 diet may work, but overall you're probably better off contracting an unsightly viral disease, which the Raider now tries to do twice a year.

The diet industry is predicated on unhealthy eating, but even what constitutes a healthy diet is clouded by spurious food industry claims backed by sponsored research. A cereal manufacturer, for instance, was forced to remove claims its breakfast improved children's concentration by 20 per cent, because they had neglected to reveal the boost was in comparison to not having breakfast at all. It's almost as if the food industry is in league with the diet industry. As if Kellogg's make Crunchy Nut Cornflakes *and* Special K. Can you imagine the brewing industry doing something similar? Trying to persuade us to drink more beer because 'Beer is good for you' or something?

Is beer good for you?
Yes.

If the brewing industry applied the same marketing ethics as the food industry, it would be considered medicine. Thankfully they haven't made that claim since Dirty South's mother was prescribed Guinness by her doctor in the glorious 1970s. If they so wished, they could have pointed to studies that show beer can make you live longer, make you thin, improve memory and creativity, boost bone density and reduce the likelihood of several illnesses. They don't need to, of course, because people will drink it regardless. And that's because it makes you feel magnificent.

Most of these studies, it should be said, are based on moderate consumption of around a pint a day, or as we like to call it, abstinence. Beer is fat-free, cholesterol-free and is low in carbohydrates. It has some of the essential nutrients that you might expect from something made from mostly plants and water, as well as antioxidants that you might not. It has had a place in the human diet for thousands of years, and not just as a means to make our friends seem funny. Beer became a vital source of safe, somewhat nutritious liquid. In the Middle Ages, to avoid the putrid water, mothers even made it for their little ones. Yummy, mummy.

Ivan Osman used to say his favourite lunch was a pint and a fag, but the modern employer frowns on even moderate drinking at lunchtime, despite the aforementioned bone density boost. In the 1970s lunchtime drinking was common and, on Fridays, expected. By the twenty-first century, the very notion of a lunch hour was under threat. Because your need for nutrition and a break is secondary to your employer's need for productivity, even on your own time. Your lunch isn't all about you, you know. Suddenly, the seventies don't seem so backward. What looked like feckless alcoholics with perms and massive collars in fact turned out to be the guardians of a Deserter way of life. Still, they're all dead now.

The potato
One of the great unspoken scandals of modern times is that the potato is not included in the British government's 'five a day' recommendation.

Tinned and frozen vegetables count towards it. Even parsnips, that can so cruelly masquerade as roasties on the plate, count towards it. And it's not as though potatoes don't contain plenty of vitamins and fibre. It's as if a deliberate evil has been perpetrated against the spud-lovers of Britain by a coalition of joyless civil servants and corrupt scientists. Why would they do such a thing?

It could be because potatoes contain toxic compounds known as glycoalkaloids. A concentration of glyco-alkaloid in potatoes can poison humans, though as the symptoms include headaches, bowel irritability and diar-rhoea it's often difficult to tell if you've been poisoned or if it's just the morning.

The answer is more straightforward: it's because they are delicious. And we mean really fucken delicious. The point being that if they told us they were good for us too we'd sit around eating them all day, every day and the economy would grind to a halt, like it did in the great oil crisis of the seventies, now thought to be directly linked to the advent of flavoured crisps.

And they are not just delicious, they are versatile, too. You can have them mashed, with butter, say. Or boiled, with butter. Or baked, with butter and cheese. You can turn them into the aforementioned crisps. They can be roasted or sauteed or formed into hash browns or pancakes or croquettes. Or even the letters of the alphabet. Try and get kale to teach you to spell and see how far you get.

Then there are chips. Lovely, wonderful, lovely chips; the apotheosis of tuber-related culinary offerings. Chips with fish, perhaps. Chips with egg. Chips with two eggs. Chips in bread, with butter again. The permutations are endless, even if they are all broadly the same. Chips are our gift to the world, despite being invented in Belgium, and though they may not be deemed to make us healthy, in fact they do better than that. They make us happy.

As a child, forced to live in the countryside by heartless, unthinking parents, the Dulwich Raider had a dream: to live somewhere that had a chip shop. No child should have to suffer the nearest chip shop being five miles away, though the NSPCC took a different view and ultimately stopped taking his calls. (Another recurring daydream of his was the discovery of a magic chip – one perfect specimen, that lasted forever. Writing this, it's tempting to conclude that he was simply underfed, or possibly just simple.)

In consequence, the Raider became adept at preparing his own chips.

'One of the greatest treats you can bestow upon yourself after a morning cocking about on the Internet,' he prattles, 'is to spend fifteen minutes peeling, slicing and shallow-frying a potato in the dripping left over from the weekend's roast.'

And yet the silence of experts is deafening.

Exercise

Exercise is one of those things that feels good once you've done it and horrific while you're doing it, like assembling flat-packed furniture or vomiting. We're not even sure it's natural. As Roxy says, you never see a lion going for a jog.

And yet the experienced libertine is wise enough to appreciate that in addition to providing a short-term hit of endorphins (essentially free drugs, remember), exercise can also ward off the dreaded 'diseases of affluence': heart disease, type 2 diabetes, obesity and, possibly, conservatism. Even low levels of exercise can improve the quality and length of one's life. And only a fool would turn down the chance of a few more sweet summers.

It is a conundrum that can drive people to distraction, particularly if you keep banging on about it while lying on the sofa covered in popcorn. The solution – as the eagle-eyed among you may have noticed about so many of our solutions – is simple. In order to make exercise palatable, you must devise a way to do it without actually noticing you're doing it. Examples include dancing, kicking a ball about or the daily struggle to do up your shoelaces.

The Raider used to keep his wine fridge on the first floor, for example, a full two flights of stairs up from the television room. Climbing that wooden hill ten times a night with his empty glass got him in such great physical condition that he once almost completed the New York Marathon (sadly, he missed the plane).

Dirty South employed a different gambit: for ten years he kept no foodstuffs on his premises. He had his kitchen removed and a pool table installed. If he wanted to eat he was obliged to walk into town to one of the fine eating establishments there, which, as luck would have it, took him right past his local. Half-life, meanwhile, keeps trim by working as a cycle courier, delivering tiny herbal and pharmaceutical packages all over town. Particularly at the weekend.

But it was our leading lady, Roxy, who stumbled upon one of the most effective gambits we've come across in this area – albeit one with a sting in the tail – when she fell for her personal trainer. We call it 'Get Fitty'.

At first he wasn't her personal trainer. He was just Jan,

a Dutch bloke she spoke to occasionally on the train, looking all handsome in his suit, with his lovely hair and everything. When she discovered he was a part-time fitness trainer, even she was surprised at how enthusiastic she suddenly became about the idea of getting in shape.

By the time May came around, she was ready to instigate her New Year's resolution and get some exercise. She bought some trainers and booked a twenty-minute session with Jan. There follows some extracts from her diary at the time:

ROXY'S FITNESS DIARY

Day 1

8 a.m. Wake with hideous hangover, coughing like an old hag. Give up smoking. Put on baggiest T-shirt even though I think it's sad and futile when fat blokes do it.

9 a.m. Meet Jan at the park. He is so bursting with sunshine and health I want to punch him in his perfect teeth. He asks a lot of questions I don't like. No, I do not smoke, thank you very much. Yes, I drink moderately. Occasionally.

He weighs me and measures me then asks me to do as many press-ups as I can. I thought I did well with three and he agreed, which made me like him a bit more. Sit-ups, though? Look, I hired you to get me fit, yet I seem to be doing all the work.

Every time I finish an exercise, he gets me to do another, immediately. I think there's something wrong with him. After the trial I am dying. It has been the hardest twenty minutes I have had since I cycled through Croydon on mushrooms. He wants me to come back for two group sessions and a one-on-one every week. And keep a food diary. I'm too tired to tell him to do one.

On the stagger back, something strange happens. A virtuous tiredness washes over me. An hour after the session, I actually feel good. I'm disappointed with myself. I go for a full English.

First Group Session

A mistake. I hate exercise and now I'm in the company of a dozen people who like it. At least it's a mixed bunch. Some lardies, some princesses who look like they eat snowflakes for breakfast and a bloke who looks like he drinks snowballs for breakfast.

Can't keep up with anyone. Shattered. What do you mean that was just the warm-up? This is mental. Impossible. Up, down, up, down. FML.

Now we're running. Actually running. I told him I hate running. I hate him again, with his easy gait and

clothes that fit. First go round I keep up with the
stragglers but – what's this? – we're going round again.
By the final stretch I am lagging far behind a monster
wobble bottom. Am too ashamed to give up.

Jan wants a word. Twat's going to sack me before I sack
him. But no, he tells me I did really well to keep going.
I'm like: 'Do you really think so?' Like I'm twelve. Must
be doing me brain in.

Jan takes apart my food diary, pointing out the
positive things first, like the salad in my kebab. Then he
tells me what I should be eating and that a diet of toast,
sandwiches and pizza is filling me up with empty calories

that are accumulating on my hips. He's a doctor now, is he? Wanker.

One-on-one

I much prefer these sessions. I'm just not a team player. Even though I have to work harder, I start to like it. I get to make him laugh. I get to punch his pads really fucking hard. He treads on my feet for my sit-ups, which raises my eyes to his bulge-level and gives me an incentive to get up there. I get to lie on my back as he stretches me. I ask him to move in.

Living with Jan

I've lost two stone. I eat well and feel fantastic. The sex is great. I'm lighter on my feet. Everything physical is easier. And yet . . .

First off, I like a glass of wine with a meal. Every meal. When we first went out, every night was a celebration. Then we got used to it. Jan started to have water. I am not getting pissed alone. Then he started doing yoga. He does it every day. He asked me to join him. He suggested I cut down on my drinking. I kicked him into touch.

The moral

Exercise is good for the body. Booze is good for the mind. Personal trainers are good for about six months.

Casual gaming

Casual gaming is a great source of incidental exercise. The Dulwich Raider is never happier than when alone in a room with a super bouncy ball or a balloon and an elaborate scoring mechanism. Things will get broken, but what is that, he reasons, compared to his health?

The age-old pleasure of kicking a tennis ball or an old Coke can along the road is well-known, but in Ireland they have a formalised game called, simply, road bowling, in which two teams take it in turns to hurl 28 oz cannon-balls along country roads in order not to notice the two-mile hike to the pub. It's not uncommon for traffic to be stopped to allow play to pass through – yes, the players have right of way. Civilisation. For shorter distances – if the pub is at the end of your road, say – we recommend boules.

Indeed, the Irish are miles ahead of the field in so many regards when it comes to taking it easy. We are reminded of the conversation between the Spanish and Irish ambassadors.

'We have a word in Spanish – "mañana" – that sums up the Spanish approach to life,' says the Spanish ambassador over some Ferrero Rocher. 'Do you have, I wonder, anything comparable in your language?'

The Irish ambassador thinks for a moment.

'Nothing, I think, that expresses such urgency,' he says.

Other casual gaming classics include Wastepaper Basket Golf, for which you simply need a wastepaper basket and balls fashioned from screwed-up newspaper wrapped in Sellotape. Some of the contortions required to get round corners are akin to pilates.

Phutt! is, excellently, played lying down, preferably in bed, and involves an orange being thrown up towards the ceiling. The object of the game is to have the orange touch the ceiling so lightly that the eponymous sound is made. Then it's your mate's go. And so on until opening time, when, depending on the landlord, the game can be continued.

Video gaming

It may not be a surprise that video gaming increases your heart rate. Indeed, the bigger surprise is that it took so many formal academic studies to reveal this, instead of anyone interested just picking up a controller and finding out for themselves.

Further studies discovered the increased heart rate, systolic and diastolic blood pressure and oxygen consumption associated with video gaming may actually be good for you.

'The increase in metabolic rate and cardiovascular stimulation is similar in magnitude to mild-intensity exercise,' concluded one report. It's worth committing this sentence to memory in order to repeat it verbatim the next time you are picked up for sitting in front of *Call of Duty* until two in the morning, drenched in sweat.

Bathing

Researchers have discovered that taking a hot bath burns as many calories as a thirty-minute walk. And on a winter night, lolling about in warm water sounds infinitely preferable to wrapping up and facing nature's sour mood.

Losing weight while horizontal is one of our favourite things, but in addition, bathing lowers inflammation and blood sugar levels after food. Regular time in the tub can also reduce blood pressure and the chance of stroke. Dirty South often claims to be tending to his exercise regime when he disappears into the bathroom with some candles, accompanied by the gentle sound of running water and the light pop of a cork. It's a wonder there's anything left of him.

Spa Break

Belief in the benefits of 'taking the waters' has been around for as long as the history of man itself, if not longer. After all, we hail from the water and perhaps it provides us with a sort of primeval comfort blanket, albeit a wet one. Ostensibly there is a feeling that existent in the waters is some form of curative power, some mysterious physical benefit for which even the finest scientific minds are unable – or as likely, unwilling – to find an explanation.

There are benefits to visiting a spa, but it's less about topping up mineral deficiencies or improving the actions of the joints than the fact that there is nothing, really, to do (see also Leisure: How to Do Fuck All). It may feel pleasant physically but it's in the mind where the benefits are most profoundly felt. And this is because, as well as the light exercise and minor medical mumbo-jumbo, visiting a spa is about the temporary opting out of life. You are essentially convalescing. You are *allowed to act ill*, to shuffle up and down in dressing gowns, lean on bannisters, reflect, pause, set your mind free until you feel ready to face the world again. Or at least lunch.

It is an experience that no aspiring loafist should miss out on. And while a stolen hour in the local council baths is not to be sniffed at, to do a spa break properly you need plenty of time and space. We're talking about a few days. A few days in a different country.

In the interests of research we sought a volunteer to do just this and write up the experience. Perhaps unsurprisingly, given his twin predilections for freebies and doing

as little as possible, the Raider was first with his hand up
– itself probably the most exercise he'd had in weeks.
This is his record.

THE RAIDER DIARIES (EXTRACT)

Day 1

What utter twunt booked me on the first flight out of
Luton airport? (Answer: me) Not only do I have to set
an alarm, it's dark when I get up and worst of all, when
I get to the airport I don't even feel like having the
traditional holiday pint. If I wasn't so tired I'd be
seething. I make a mental note to fire my secretary,
before remembering I don't have one.

Nevertheless, I have the presence of mind to procure a
bottle of Scotch on the plane. I have no idea what I'll be
doing on a Slovakian 'Spa Island' for three days, but I
do know I won't be doing it without whisky.

At Bratislava airport I am met by Marek who drives
me the ninety or so kilometres to Piešťany, Slovakia's
most famous spa town, while I grab some zeds on his
shoulder. After an hour we turn off the motorway and
drive through a huge hotel complex that sits within the
stately grounds of Spa Island, a resort that was once
popular during the communist regime and which is now

reinventing itself as a destination for knackered
foreigners.

At reception I am informed that, as a special guest, I
am being upgraded to the five-star Thermia Palace, the
Art Nouveau resort showpiece. I make a note to rehire
my secretary, or at least stand him (me) a drink.

A porter takes my bags and I am given a piece of
paper with my room number on it. On the way up I
spot people wandering about in towelling gowns, some
of them looking quite unwell. There are bewildering
signs and directions for therapies, sanatoria, a 'White
Room' and the doctor's. The doctor's? I realise with a
start that while from the outside it looks like a hotel
(and to be fair, I've already logged a sign to the bar), the
place in which I am standing resembles, more than
anything, a hospital.

I am surprised to find that what I thought was my
room looks more like a waiting room, and even more
surprised to find it contains a desk with a stern,
bespectacled woman sitting behind it.

'Come,' she beckons. I take a seat opposite her and
there begins a series of difficult and/or incomprehensible
questions:

'Accident?'

'Pardon?'

'Accident?'

'No thanks,' I say and she writes something down.

'Height?'

I feel on firmer ground here.

'Five foot ten and three-quarters,' I say, trying to affect the air of a man who could take or leave the three-quarters of an inch.

'Height centimetres?' she says.

'Centimetres?' I say, and she gives a little sigh.

'Blood,' she says.

'I'm fine, thanks,' I say. Another little sigh and she gets up to take my blood pressure.

'Pressure,' she confides.

'Tell me about it,' I say.

Eventually she is finished and she ushers me through another door to see the doctor, who asks me all the same questions in a slightly different order. From here I am whisked into lunch in the grand dining hall, where I am delighted to be offered a glass of red wine at my table, perhaps confirming recent reports in the press that a glass of red wine is as good for you as an hour in the gym.

'Leave the bottle,' I say, 'I'm training for the marathon.' And I watch heavy snow begin to fall through the enormous dining room windows while I await my schnitzel.

By the time I am issued with my room key I am able

to sip whisky from a tooth mug on my balcony and behold a veritable winter wonderland. An hour later I find myself wading waist-deep through hot mud, alone in a giant otherworldly dome, after which I am wrapped in a towel and left in the dark for a snooze. C'mon, you five-star hospitals!

Day 2

I awake feeling magnificent, which is amplified by a glass of bubbles for breakfast. Oddly, I go for a long walk in the snow.

Two treatments today, one in the morning and one after lunch. My first is a massage and my masseur is a short, fop-haired beast whose cragged face has seen far better days. He cracks his knuckles and gets to work. As he gets up close to work on my torso I can smell alcohol and cigarettes on his breath. Not quite the aromatherapeutic experience I was expecting, but nonetheless not unpleasant; like having a rubdown in a distillery, from my father.

Afterwards he orders me to drink water in order to 'flush out the toxins' – like that's a good thing – and then sends me to lounge in an enormous sulphurous outside pool, like a basking whale. The steam rises from the water and the snow clouds momentarily clear to reveal bright sunshine which glints through the autumnal browns of the surrounding woodland. It's really rather lovely.

There is something to be said for spending some time in a different element. At the very least, it's unusual. I think about some of the other elements. Earth, wind . . . and fire, is it? Fire doesn't sound much fun, to be honest. And I wouldn't fancy spending a day in the wind. It would be like holidays in Wales all over again and my earache would probably come back.

I survey my fellow bathers. I am the youngest person in the pool by about thirty years. It strikes me as entirely possible that no guests have ever had sex in this place. I try to imagine them having sex. I try to imagine myself having sex with them. I leave the pool.

After lunch I sit in the changing room and wait for my second treatment with fellow spa guest, Omar from Kuwait. A blonde Scarlett Johansson lookalike comes in and looks over at us.

'Get undressed and follow please,' she breathes, and we both get up. 'Not you,' she says to me. 'You wait here.' Omar gives me a little wink. Shortly afterwards my guy from yesterday arrives.

'Come,' he barks and I follow him down the corridor. Twenty minutes later I am naked, covered in mud and being hosed down by a stocky brute in a butcher's coat.

Day 3

Relaxed and yet exhausted I sleep through dinner and awake ravenous at 1 a.m.

The hotel kitchen is closed so I wander out onto the island where there are some men night-fishing on the opposite bank. I briefly consider fashioning a sign but realise I have no idea how to write 'Please fetch chips!' in Slovakian.

After a fulsome breakfast, Omar asks me if I would care for a game of tennis and I hear myself saying, 'Yes.' After lunch we play pétanque. Then we go for another massage, during which I conceive the fantastical idea of recording heavy metal versions of Ennio Morricone tunes. I shall call it 'Horricone'. Oh, yes.

I realise that, largely due to there being little else to do, I am not only becoming fit, but my cloudy mind is beginning to clear. I am having ideas. If only I was here for a bit longer.

'How long are you here for?' I ask Omar.

'The usual,' he says. 'Three weeks.'

Lucky bugger. To console myself I pour two fingers of whisky and walk into the woods to smoke the hash I smuggled through customs in the lining of my glasses case. The way I look at it, if you don't have any toxins in your body, how can you flush them out?

Grooming

It's not just the committed layabout that finds grooming a chore. No one in their right mind looks forward to clipping their hideous toenails or crawling out of bed for a shave. And yet we advocate that due care and attention is taken with one's appearance.

What is this bullcrap? you may ask. *Why can't I just let myself go like Johnny Depp or Helena Bonham Carter?* And we would respectfully remind you that grooming is a symbol of humanity, a sign you are not a sociopath. Yes, you are on the lookout for a good time all the time, but you are not some sort of savage. Allowing your hair to grow unkempt and your clothes to become infused with weeks of body odour is only one step away from piddling yourself at the table because you can't be arsed to go to the toilet, liberating as that can be.

The truth is, once the grooming stops, it's all over.

The Dulwich Raider learned this the hard way as a postgraduate. He'd read somewhere that the requirement to wash one's hair was a myth perpetuated by the shampoo industry and that, left to its own devices, hair *will actually clean itself*. Not being a scientist – indeed, far from it – and, like all students, being a bit pushed for time and money, he decided the path of least resistance was simply to believe this. He determined to no longer waste valuable seconds in the shower.

Some weeks into the first term he was chuffed to be invited to tea in the college rooms of one of the most attractive girls in his year. As he walked down the corridor towards her room he heard his name mentioned and stood for a moment to listen further at the crack in the door.

'He seems really nice, doesn't he?' the hot girl was saying *about him*, and the Raider caught his breath.

'Good-looking, too,' replied her friend, and went on, 'But have you smelled his hair?'

'Yes,' said the hot girl. 'It fucking stinks.'

After an uncomfortable afternoon sitting as close as possible to the open window, he resumed hair washing the next morning. But the damage was done – she got off with some maths twat from Imperial.

Relieve Stress . . .

Balance, as we have seen, is a key component of a happy, healthy, unproductive life. People often talk about the 'work/life balance' – an equilibrium that is so sadly lacking in many modern societies. The placement of 'work' in that phrase is significant. It suggests you must fit your life around your work, rather than the preferred configuration in which work fits around your life. If anything, we advocate a 'pleasure/life balance'. Fit your life around your pleasures. There, that's better.

Making work the focus of your existence is simply dangerous to your health and the reason for that is often stress-related. Unless you're a firefighter, in which case it is dangerous because of fire.

The main causes of stress are: a) work, which we are against; b) money, which we wish to receive without resorting to a) and c) poor relationships, which we strive to ameliorate through self-improvement, not to mention a greater focus on leisure, pleasure and entertaining company.

Put simply, if you're stressed, you are probably giving too much of a toss about something. Humans are not designed to be stressed; we're designed to lie about, eating pancakes and stimulating each other's mucus membranes in a perverse polymorphous free-for-all. 'Fight or flight' responses should be sparse, one-off events, not how we feel whenever the phone rings.

It is no coincidence that the origin of the word 'business' lies in the Old English word for anxiety – *bisignis*. Follow our approach to the world of work and you will find that you don't experience the levels of stress that afflict so many. Work will no longer keep you up at night. And if you've been paying attention, it will barely get you up in the morning, either.

But you can find yourself stressed in all sorts of situations, some of which we are able to offer solutions to here.

Public speaking

Conventional wisdom has it that if you have to give a speech in public it can help to imagine the audience naked. Ivan Osman prefers to imagine them dead, and that he's been living alone on a dying planet for millennia, which gives him great comfort.

Half-life, part-time purveyor of petrifying poetry, takes to the stage dressed as a pastor or an Italian road cop, among other things. Is this, we wondered, a technique to reduce nerves, to provide a mask to hide behind? Turns out it's just great for meeting ladies.

Relationships

Nothing makes you feel at ease like having a doting partner draped round your shoulders, right? But if you're single, how do you go about getting one without inducing more stress?

One quick fix is to invent one. The Dulwich Raider had an imaginary girlfriend for most of his first year of university, until she dumped him for being too needy – admittedly a low point for him. Splendidly, he claims girls then took pity on him and jumped his bones all summer.

On the other hand, many cite a relationship itself as a cause of stress. In affairs of the heart it is not only respectful to be honest with one another, it can actually alleviate tension. If you find yourself falling out of love with your partner, for example, just tell them.

'I'm going off you a bit so I think we should start seeing better people' is an excellent wake-up call, particularly in a marriage. If this doesn't work, once again the answer is blindingly obvious: get rid of them. The stress of a break-up is nothing compared to years of sharing your life with someone who uses a metal utensil in a non-stick pan.

Divorce

Divorce, in our view, should really be a time of great joy. You have realised a relationship has reached its end and you are expressing that, through a lawyer. The main reason people find divorce stressful is that it requires dealing with someone you no longer love, or quite possibly hate. But isn't the end of something difficult or unpleasant worth celebrating? Don't you smile in the last five minutes of a workday, or as the curtain falls on an evening of musical theatre with Auntie Dave?

Of course, if you are parting with the love of your life, you are bound to be terribly sad. But if you have reached the point of the decree absolute, the best you can do is reflect on the good times and be glad you had them. Indeed, Half-life enjoys an extravagant commemoration of his divorce every year.

'Sod Christmas. Divorce Day is the most wonderful time of the year,' he beams, though possibly only because that's when his ex-wife takes him out for some posh nosh to celebrate her good fortune.

Money

Money problems are renowned for being one of the biggest causes of anxiety.

Ivan Osman's solution, when faced with sinking slowly

into the financial mire, was to rebrand life's money matters as a complex real-world online role-playing game. Being a keen gamer, he was soon flipping credit cards, redeeming vouchers, optimising savings accounts and asking for rises until he got where he is today (an eight-bed waterfront mansion in Long Island, NY).

Faced with insurmountable debts, another solution is to move house without leaving a forwarding address, then move again rather quickly, and then leave the country, as Dirty South did when fleeing a place we shall call Astraulia. He even dumped the hire car he was driving at the airport, the half-eaten pizza he was supposed to be delivering cold on the passenger seat. Almost everyone you know who has left the country suddenly did so for this reason. Which, now we mention it, does make us wonder about Osman.

So, stress can creep up on us in many different situations. Sometimes we may be able to address it head on, at other times we must simply gravitate towards those things that tend to ease suffering, like Scampi Fries.

The importance of laughter

Laughter is known to trigger healthy physical and emotional responses in the body, and we're not even joking. It strengthens the immune system, enhances our mood, diminishes pain and relaxes our bodies. But where can we find this free health supplement? TV and live comedy are there for us, but surrounding yourself with funny friends is best. If you're lucky enough to have a few of those, make sure you see plenty of them. They're better than doctors.

'And even nurses,' adds Dirty South.

But perhaps your friends are serious types who, while reliable and possibly even kind, are a bit hard going. Laughter is not something you can simply invent. It's a gift from human to human, spontaneously scattered within earshot, before drifting off, having delivered its happy health boost. We laugh at unexpected responses and witty punchlines. But we also laugh at people slipping over or tripping up. In the absence of hilarious friends, try hanging around uneven paving. You could even add a trip hazard of your own, such as a rake or a precariously balanced bucket of paint, and simply wait for passers-by to have an accident. Should you evade capture by your new, clumsy, rage-filled friend, you'll laugh so much you'll live forever, probably.

When we were children, laughter was never far away. The giggling was uncontrollable. A simple fart sound could leave us in helpless hysterics. Sadly, laughter decreases in inverse proportion to age. As we get older, we become harder to amuse. But laughter is contagious, so if you can't find a funny friend, at least find a good, easy laugher and you'll soon be releasing endorphins into your own system, experiencing mild euphoria and dulling pain, all without a prescription.

Sunlight

Sunlight is nature's way of reducing stress and another reason why afternoon pub crawls were invented. As we have seen, pub crawls are not just about drinking, they're also about health – something we may always somehow have known but have not hitherto had the scientific evidence to back up. Now studies are ten a penny showing that sunlight boosts our levels of serotonin – a neurotransmitter which improves mood, sleep and memory.

Furthermore, despite being a known cause of sandals, sunlight allows our bodies to create vitamin D, which has a protective effect against multiple diseases, including cancer. Research from the University of Pittsburgh and Carnegie Mellon University suggests that sunlight also affects not just the moods of patients undergoing surgery, but also their pain medication usage. They found that patients who were placed in bright rooms were able to take less medication than patients in dim rooms. Or, one assumes, take the same amount and feel utterly stupendous, which would be our approach.

Gardening

Nobody knows for sure why people do it, but gardening, as we saw in 'Home', can be an effective means of relaxation, of regaining control and in turn, of reducing stress and improving general health.

A recent study in the Netherlands showed that those who engage in gardening reduce their levels of the stress hormone cortisol more quickly than those who, for example, read a book. Though this may depend on the type of book you're reading. We've seen some of those Dutch books.

Regular gardening is also acknowledged to stave off dementia and reduce symptoms of depression, though the side effects of this are that you find yourself listening to *Gardeners' Question Time* or tutting at farming inaccuracies in *The Archers*, which is, ironically, both mad and depressing.

Research at the University of Colorado Boulder in the United States even suggests that the harmless bacteria *Mycobacterium vaccae* commonly found in soil increases the release and metabolism of serotonin in parts of the brain that control cognitive function and mood. As we've always known deep down, it feels good to be dirty.

And so, like plants emerging from a barren winter into the growing season, reducing stress can allow your confidence to flourish. You are a flower, free from the frost of anxiety and ready to blossom. Or at least have a go on some fertiliser.

. . . Build Confidence

Confidence is not a prerequisite for enjoying your life, but a lack of it could cause you to make life choices that make you unhappy. Friends, family and media can exert pressure on you to conform or to take a path that may not be for you, and it is important to be able to rebuff them and follow your desires.

If you do not, you face life as a square peg in a round hole, grimly aware that you could and should be doing something more appropriate with your existence. This kind of situation erodes confidence and, in turn, your self-esteem – the ability to love yourself (not like that). As self-esteem and confidence reduce, stress increases, which is exhausting, forces you into bad decisions and – in a circle so vicious it has teeth – thereby further reduces your confidence.

As our lawyers are really very keen to make clear, we are not qualified doctors, but nevertheless we feel compelled to pass on what we know of how to build confidence. Your confidence can be undermined by many things, particularly as the borderline-lunatic surety of youth begins to slip through your fingers. Take care to nurture it, as, after your credit card, it's your most important asset.

Friends

It is our contention that if you are lacking in confidence you may be hanging out with the wrong people. Friends should make you feel better about yourself, not worse. There's no point hanging out with the great and the good if they get on your subconscious tits with all their charisma and success. Nor should negative, critical friends be allowed to impinge on your psyche. No, you need to find some new friends – a nice gang of lovable fools. People who make you look and feel good.

Physical appearance

Body fascism is the cause of much misery, but there is no doubt that one's physical appearance can be a crucial factor in one's self-esteem. Our view is that if you're happy to be fat and ugly, for example, there is nothing wrong in being so. But if it plays on your mind, then consider losing some weight and just being ugly. What is paramount is your happiness.

Sex

Nothing boosts our self-esteem like a damn good seeing to – and not just because it requires rigorous exercise for up to thirty seconds. It means someone *desires* us and is prepared to express that physically, possibly without some of their clothes. Sometimes your need for each other is so urgent that you don't even put your things in the laundry basket; you just toss your clothes on the floor like some kind of demented animal, your inhibitions gone, along with your socks. Yes, sex is right up there with a good old pat on the back. If only we could bottle it. 'Sex: get that freshly fucked feeling!'

The pep talk

Bigging yourself up can work wonders. Each morning the Dulwich Raider reputedly stands in front of the mirror and repeats, 'I am Viscount Raider, landed gentry, 749th in line to the throne and one of just ten people in the UK with a Gold Tastecard' before going back to bed for an hour, probably mumbling something about chips.

Pepping yourself up is fine, but resist the temptation to pep up others – everyone will think you're a bore. As Half-life puts it, 'By all means reach for the stars, because if you miss, at least you'll be fucking miles away from me with your motivational bullshit.'

Here are some ideas for celebrating your special powers – the things that make you amazing. Memorise them and repeat them to yourself whenever confidence deserts you:

- I have the ability to remain underwater for short periods of time
- I can fly (for even shorter periods of time)
- I can change TV channels without getting up
- I can turn any foodstuff into fecal matter
- I can read upside down, albeit not as well as the right way up
- I can occasionally predict the past

Crutches

If all else fails, let's not forget drugs and alcohol. Treat yourself. After the first glass of Merlot you will feel nicely refreshed. After the second bottle you'll be positively imperial and ready to get up for work.

Comfort eating gets a bad rap, but there is nothing wrong with a little bit of what makes you happy and you should not beat yourself up about it. A simple bacon sarnie, a nice cheeseburger or a toad in the hole is absolutely fine if it cheers you up. Although they will, of course, all give you cancer.

For pudding lovers it's worth remembering that

'stressed' is 'desserts' spelled backwards. Thus it follows that the eating of sugary foods can actually reverse your stress. (We did say we're not doctors.)

In conclusion, let us recall the accepted wisdom that everyone needs to be liked. Well, the hard truth is, not everyone likes you. Some people think you're a shallow attention-seeker who prioritises your own happiness above all else, like your mother once wrote in that Christmas card. Once you realise this, you can relax and stop trying to please everyone. The irony is, people will then like you more. Funny old world.

We need more than booze alone
Aim for pre-obese
There is no such thing as free gout
'Weightwatchers' contains the word 'twat'
Beer is good for you
Hair does not 'clean itself'
You are a flower
Get that freshly fucked feeling

DEATH

'Death is the last enemy: once we've got past that I think everything will be alright.'

– Alice Thomas Ellis, author

♦ What Happens When You Die ♦ What Happens When You Nearly Die ♦ Dealing with Bereavement ♦ The Top Five Regrets of the Dying

'The only certainties in life are death and taxes,' wrote Benjamin Franklin, who couldn't have foreseen the advent of Facebook – notably shy when it comes to taxes and where your profile can live on forever as an online memorial to your life, or perhaps cats doing the darnedest things. But life is not our primary concern in this chapter. That is death.

The fact of the matter is, death – particularly our own death – is very hard to talk about. This is partly due to the fact that we've never done it. We're not used to dying. We're used to waking up first thing every morning, which is bad enough.

It may be tempting to consider death as the ultimate act of Desertion. After all, you get to leave behind your debts, there's no more work or responsibilities and, best of all, you can skip Henry and Octavia's dinner party on Saturday. But whenever you tire of life – perhaps at the prospect of another thirty years struggling to pay the rent, or maybe you've splashed hot fat on your new top – remember this: it is better than the other options. For we are pleasure-seekers, and without the ability to draw breath, there is no pleasure to be had: no hot tea or sunshine, no art or wine, no giggles, no sex, no *butter*.

Some would have you believe that, somehow, you do not die but that your spirit goes on forever, like that bottle of amaretto at the back of the kitchen cabinet. This may well be so (it isn't), but whatever heaven is like, there has never been a depiction of it that looks fun, let alone acceptable. Tranquillity, celestial choirs and angels? No thank you. If we were told: 'And lo, there will be cake. And some half-decent MDMA. And everyone will fancy you,' we could imagine taking a keen interest in the after-life. But a life of deferred pleasure, just to hang out with the choral crowd, has limited appeal.

Death is perhaps easier to face when we realise that life has no meaning. And while this may be difficult for some to accept, it's much better than it having a meaning of which you disapprove. We're not here to work hard, or suffer, or prove ourselves in the eyes of an almighty being, nor even to be kind and help others. We're here to fuck about. Quite literally. And anything else is up to you.

But listen to us, going on about life again. Onward. To death.

What Happens When You Die

Odd as it may seem to you, sat there at the very centre of the universe, only two things happen when you die:

1. People who knew you will feel sad that you've gone. Or, if you were a twat, chuffed.
2. People will read your phone messages aloud to one another. (Yes, it's worth bucking your ideas up in this department.)

Apart from this, everything just chunters on as normal without you. Almost as if you weren't there.

What Happens When You Nearly Die

Many believe that near-death experiences, such as myocardial infarction, suffocation or sitting through two hours of experimental mime, can grant a glimpse into the afterlife. People who have been clinically dead and then resuscitated variously report meetings with God or Death, great feelings of serenity or understanding, or of discovering an unconditional love. On the other hand, when you think about it, it could all have been a lovely dream.

Recently, while undergoing a minor procedure to remove an ingrown toenail, the Dulwich Raider almost left us. Partly out of semi-professional interest, and partly in order to prevent him telling us about it at every given opportunity, we asked him to record his experiences, which we reproduce here in an unexpurgated form:

THE RAIDER DIARIES (EXTRACT)

King's Hospital, Camberwell
It hadn't started well.

'Take it easy, Morris, nothing to worry about,' the doctor had said. 'It's a straightforward procedure. There's really no need to panic.'

'But my name's not Morris,' I said.

'No, I'm Morris,' he said.

And so the last thing I can clearly remember of the real world is insisting upon a full anaesthetic. Local anaesthetics, for which one requires the courage to remain awake and possibly even watch the surgery are, in my view, the preserve of the brave: Royal Marines, for example, or women. It's not my game.

The doctor administered something quite sublime and before I could ask him if it was available in Boots I could feel myself slipping into oblivion, where I remained quite happily for a few moments, doing Sudoku.

The next thing I knew, my bodily spirit, entirely without permission, decided to ascend to the ceiling and view the proceedings from there. I saw myself lying on the bed. Jeez, I looked tired. And was my hair really that long? And yet still, somehow, I remained gorgeous. The flowers my wife bought me sat in the vase on my utility table, next to a family bag of Revels. I hope the nurse doesn't snaffle one of them, I thought to myself, and if she does, I hope she gets a coffee one.

I felt something tugging at my hand. I looked round to see a fair-haired winged creature, like a giant bug, pawing at me.

'Jesus Christ!' I ejaculated.

'Close,' said the creature. 'Come, I wish to show you a bright light, at the end of a long tunnel.'

Unable to think of an excuse, I was led down a corridor, past Renal, Cardiology and the little shop where I'd noticed they were doing Walkers Crisps Grab Bags for half price. That is unbeatable value.

'What is that you're carrying?' I asked the blonde monster.

'It is a small, portable harp, known as a "medieval" harp,' wittered the creature.

'Could be worse, it could be a fucking ukulele,' I said, trying to make conversation. 'I call them fuckuleles.'

The gargoyle didn't respond. Sure enough, at the end of another long corridor a bright light came into view and my feathered friend began to fly a little more urgently.

'Do you mind not flapping so hard,' I said. 'My hair's going all over the place.'

'Maybe you should have had a trim,' said the freak, with just the tiniest hint of needle.

'Are you a boy or a girl?' I asked, and immediately recalled being asked the same question as a child by an elderly paedophile in a Clacton-on-Sea amusement arcade. My life was flashing before my eyes, or at least, my flashers were.

'I am a servant of the Light,' replied the beast, as we became all but consumed by the intense brightness.

'And what do you wish of me, o non-gendered winged one?'

'Could you pass me up that bulb? Some arsehole's put a seventy-watt halogen in here when it should have been a twenty-eight.' The spell was broken.

'Twenty-eight watts?' I said. 'You mean, sufficient lumens for a regular desk lamp?'

'Exactly,' said the angel, who I now recognised as a hospital maintenance operative.

'Are we dead?' I asked

'Might as well be. £9.50 an hour? You're having a laugh, aren't you? I spend that on parking. Unless I can get Ronnie's ticket, but I'm not always on the next shift. Why would I be? That would be too simple. And if there's one thing I've learned, it's that them upstairs don't like anything to be simple. I'm telling you, when I first started here . . .'

I was alive, and yet I longed for death.

_____

And there we will leave the Raider's story, as we are no longer certain of its relevance. We suppose the moral of the story is, if you are going to have a near-death experience, at least try to keep it interesting.

Dealing with Bereavement

Having established that your own death is really nothing to do with you at all, you will be relieved to hear that this section is all about number one again. Death is, curiously, a fact of life and we are all likely to experience the loss of friends and loved ones at some point (unless we die early and suddenly in a terrible accident, in which case we may just get away with it). Grief at this kind of loss will inevitably take the edge off your day and may even, we're sorry to say, persist.

There is, of course, plenty of help on coping with grief to be found on the Internet. Just type in 'coping with the loss of a husband' – or wife, mother, grandparent or whatever – into Google, and click 'I'm feeling lucky'.

It is generally acknowledged among psychologists and counsellors that there are several stages of grief – variously five, seven or even nine. No one needs nine stages of grief so, in order to save time, we've got it down to three:

Stage 1: Boozing

First comes the overwhelming urge to get munted. While this has been shown to have no lasting benefit, boy does it make you feel better while you're doing it.

After turning off his mother's life-support machine (under medical supervision, we should add, to prevent the police reopening the case) the Dulwich Raider popped into the Wheatsheaf on his way home to be greeted by Roxy, Spider, Dirty South et al., who plied him with drink and then, splendidly, all took the following day off to take him to the races where more soothing Guinness was liberally applied.

'It really was tremendous behaviour on their part,' he recalls. 'Plus I won £13.50 on the Placepot, which also helped a great deal.'

Stage 2: Smoking

The next stage in recovery is usually to take up smoking again, which feels so right that you question why you ever gave up in the first place. Others may take it up for the first time, which only goes to underline our capacity to seek out new, exciting experiences even when we're under the cosh.

Stage 3: Binge eating

The final stage in this 'What's the bloody point of it all?' frenzy is to knock the diet on the head and buy yourself a deep fat fryer and a chocolate fountain. Coupled with an overwhelming desire to lie down and look at the ceiling for hours, it is likely this will lead to a little extra luggage around the waist. Do not fret, just enjoy yourself. Eventually, due to the passage of time, the urge to binge will pass, to be replaced with simple overindulgence, like in the old days.

You may have heard that 'time heals all wounds', which sounds like it might be true but doesn't tell the whole story. We don't forget loved ones, but we feel the wound of loss more keenly when it is fresh because we have nothing else on our minds. It is not time *per se* that heals, but what we do in that time. Talking to friends and strangers, pole dancing, spending the night in a skip, hell, even going to a pub quiz . . . The more you do, the better you'll feel. We thrive on stimulus. More than ever we need to celebrate variety and to appreciate everyday life, the wonders of the ordinary – it's what keeps us special.

In times of sadness, it's worth remembering that our capacity for distraction is not pointless. Without it we could become trapped in grief. Or worse, work. During these difficult times, we have noted two further coping mechanisms which it may be useful to bear in mind.

Remember the bad times

There's a tendency to think the best of the recently passed, to 'not speak ill of the dead'. That's only natural. The graveside is no place to remind the congregation of the deceased's tight-fisted, humourless ways, much less their halitosis. But it can be helpful to the healing process to remember the dearly departed's shortcomings, as the Dulwich Raider found after the loss of a dear friend.

As the Raider inconsolably polished off the mini-burgers, Dirty South reminded him of the time the deceased got him arrested outside a Soho bar, pointing the finger in his direction in order to deflect attention from his own guilt. To make matters worse, he then tried to make amends by bringing the Raider's jacket to the police station, thinking he would be shivering in a cell. Unfortunately he forgot to empty the pockets of the Raider's weed.

'Your mate's here,' the arresting officer had said, with a chuckle, tossing the Raider his coat. 'And he brought your drugs.'

The memories came flooding back and soon the Raider made the journey from the pit of grief to having to be restrained from slapping the corpse, settling in the end for flicking peanuts into the coffin, which cheered him up enormously.

Just say yes

When a loved one dies, we feel bereft. We wonder how we can go on without them. We consider our own mortality along with the search for meaning and various life insurance documents. Friends will sense this so, instead of soldiering on with mere sympathy for support, try saying 'Yes' to the question, 'Is there anything I can do to help?'

Say, 'Yes, I could really use a massage.' Or, 'Yes, I could really do with a nice holiday. Somewhere warm. But not too warm, mind.' Or ask for a car. Or a month rent-free. Or at least a contribution to the three stages of grief, in the form of a pint, a fag and a souvlaki.

It won't bring your loved one back, but at least they won't have died in vain.

Funerals

There's a tendency to think of the funeral as the point of acceptance; the jumping-off point for moving on. But it is not the end of mourning. Nor is it the beginning of the end. Nor is it even the beginning of the end of the beginning of the end. It is, though, as Spider says, a great place to pull.

Funerals can often be the best party of the year, which is why it's always good to make lots of friends, the older the better. It's even better if you make bad friends because then you're not even that bothered when they die. You can just enjoy the finger buffet before everyone gets happy and flirty.

Top Five Regrets of the Dying

And so we return to the regrets of the dying, as mentioned in the introduction and collated by Bronnie Ware in her book *The Top Five Regrets of the Dying*. While her findings, recorded from her conversations with her palliative care patients, may not assist you directly in preparing for death, they may prove useful in determining how you live before that moment comes, which amounts to the same thing.

1. **I wish I'd had the courage to live a life true to myself, not the life others expected of me.**

   Ware wrote that, 'Once we acknowledge that limited time is remaining . . . we are less driven by ego or what other people think.' It's an important lesson, and one that we should reinforce to those we love. Try adding the message: 'Enjoy your special day, but bear in mind death awaits' to birthday cards (or cakes).

Human existence is littered with unfulfilled dreams and dashed expectations, not least due to our meek acquiescence to the wishes and beliefs of others. Difference, nonconformity and passion seem to be discouraged rather than celebrated, and yet without the courage of those prepared to stand up for what they believe in, we'd still be proclaiming that the sun orbits the Earth, that the Earth is flat, or that tomatoes are some kind of fruit.

The lesson of this regret is clear: do more of the things that call you, things that you believe in, even if those things conflict with what your parents, friends, teachers or bosses have in mind for you. It doesn't matter if that activity is best for you or not; having your own experiences, making up your own mind and, in particular, making your own mistakes is the most visceral and efficient way to learn both what it is that you want from life and what it is that you don't.

Like Copernicus and Galileo before him, the Dulwich Raider was not tempted by the graduate fast-track into the banking industry that his father had planned for him, preferring to pursue part-time work and full-time dreaming. Pressed by his father as to what it was exactly he proposed to do instead, he merely grinned to himself and mumbled a vulgar English idiom synonymous with 'nothing'.

'Son,' replied Raider Snr. 'More men have landed on the Moon than have landed on that barren island.' And with that he left the room. The Raider pondered this unexpected and oddly poetic wisdom. It stayed with him. Maybe he should get a job after all, he thought, and he agreed to a hellish three-month internship with NatWest.

But this unfortunate period only served to reinforce the Raider's innate sense that he didn't belong in a suit and tie, not to mention instil a lifelong loathing of the office, of routine and of mornings. He was set fair on the path to work-shy bliss.

It later transpired his father had thought he'd said 'Rockall'.

2. I wish I hadn't worked so hard

Look, there's no point beating about the bush with this one – we told you so. If you can't quit your job, do less of it. Reduce your hours, your days or your commute and you can reduce stress, ill-health and that feeling of pointlessness. If you're going to feel pointless, at least feel it in a hammock looking at the stars or in the bay window of a seaside pub.

Do less work and gradually you will remember who you are and what you liked doing in the old days, before you became a unique taxpayer code. Next thing you know, you'll be reading a book or humming a little tune, like you're happy or something.

So, before working too hard becomes a regret for you, act immediately. Hesitation is your enemy, particularly if you find yourself hesitating for the next decade. Indeed, it is (possibly) worth recalling here that 'hesitate' is an anagram of 'eat shite'.

3. I wish I'd had the courage to express my feelings

Suppressed feelings don't disappear, they simply manifest themselves in other ways: anger, depression or boils, usually. Every time you bite your tongue to keep the peace, a little bit of who you are dies, along with your tongue.

Many Britons would rather die than speak their mind, unlike Americans, who will frequently do so while looking you *straight in the eye*, of all things. It's not that we fear disagreement in the UK, nor even conflict, necessarily. We just don't like people looking at us. To avoid this deathbed remorse of unfound courage, we must summon the confidence of royalty.

'I simply look down upon everyone as if they were scum,' said Half-life, when asked how he generates such searing honesty. A handy tactic for work conferences, but less so for meeting your partner's parents. Though Half-life would strongly disagree.

But letting your feelings be known feels better immediately, regardless of the outcome. And ultimately avoids any unnecessary longing to change the past. Why not engage, say your piece and encourage dialogue in order to reach accord with your adversary? Or, failing that, you could just call them names. Perhaps when they've left the room.

If it is your nature to be timid and accommodating, to bow to the will of others despite your true feelings – particularly the ones with loud boomy voices – remember the words spoken by Julius Caesar in Shakespeare's eponymous play:

Cowards die many times before their deaths;
The valiant never taste of death but once.

Having said that, Caesar was savagely murdered by colleagues for expressing his true feelings, so there's also something to be said for keeping schtum.

4. I wish I had stayed in touch with my friends

The average person interacts with 80,000 people in their lifetime, unless they're an air hostess, when it's closer to 20 million and explains why they may fail to respond when you ask them for an extra potato with lunch, even with your best smile. And of these 80,000 people, anthropologists suggest you will call about 150 of them friends at any given time.

As we move through life, heading off to university, perhaps, starting a new job or moving to a new city, we tend to acquire new friends and shed the old ones, particularly the racist ones. And the ones who set fire to things.

But it's drifting apart from friends to whom we were

once close that is referred to in this regret. We're ambivalent on this point. Yes, your friends are important, but is it your fault that they decided to move to Wiltingshire? Are you seriously expected to jump on a train on a weeknight just to admire their new stair carpet, when you could be out making new friends?

A better option here is to throw a big annual bash, to which you can invite all your old mates and make a big to-do on Facebook about how much you're looking forward to seeing all the old faces. Then, if they can't make it, it's their lookout. And something they will regret terribly, when they are dying.

Roxy found herself in the shadow of these last two regrets when her friend Cathy announced she was moving to Sydney. After describing her magnificent new harbourside home, she implored her, 'You will come and see us, won't you, Rox?'

She was on the verge of confirming when she remembered she had not gone to see Cathy a single time since she moved twenty miles out of town, three years ago. Indeed, she only saw her when Cathy came to London.

'Of course I won't,' she said, invoking the honesty that combats Regret No. 3. Three years later Cathy moved back to the UK and made a point of seeking out her truthful friend. A happy ending, of sorts, though Cathy now lives in Exeter, which may as well be on the other side of the world.

5. I wish that I had let myself be happier

All our lives we are taught to be proper, better, disciplined and correct. No one ever tells us simply to be happy. It's as if our happiness is considered almost the enemy of righteousness, whereas in fact it is more likely to be its parent. Who is more likely to care about others, to be empathetic, to be determined to give as well as take – the happy, or the miserable?

It's interesting that this regret suggests there is an element of volition in happiness. Can you choose to be happy? We're not sure, but it's got to be worth a try. The Deserter's default position is to look for positives, and if they do not present themselves naturally, then it is possible we need to realign our thresholds.

When Spider burst into tears at the prospect of a rail replacement bus in the rain on a day trip to Margate one Sunday, it contrasted starkly with the Dulwich Raider's mood: he was already relishing a good sit-down and the meditative benefits of a rain-soaked Garden of England slipping past the coach windows, aided perhaps by the heavy pocket-feel of his trusty hip flask and the prospect of a Premier League double-header. The only thing that was letting him down was the company.

'But what is there to be positive about?' sobbed Spider, as the Raider wondered if he could lose him at Herne Bay.

After intensive research we've narrowed these 'positives' down to six basic areas: love-sex, booze-drugs, sport-games, nature-wow, people-lols and art. If you can't find something in that lot to either improve the moment or give you something to look forward to, then we just hope we never get stuck opposite you at dinner. Indeed, if this is the case we would suggest that it is possible you are actually choosing *not* to be happy, perhaps out of guilt, or anger, or fear. Banish these interlopers! They are the enemies of expansiveness, the gaolers of your inner Deserter.

Remember, beyond illness, divorce, depression or debt there is a fresh crab sandwich and a sunny day waiting for you (except maybe in Margate). At the end of the working day there is a pint. At the end of the journey home there is a cup of tea. At the end of the day there is a bed, a dream and, if you're lucky, a cuddle in the morning. Allow it.

Life is better than the other options
Send better phone messages
Your death is nothing to do with you
Just say yes
Check pockets for drugs
Funerals are great for pulling
'Hesitate' is an anagram of 'eat shite'

AFTERWORD

'I tell you, we are here on Earth to fart around,
and don't let anybody tell you different.'

– Kurt Vonnegut, author

If you have turned straight to this chapter then you're
either a natural Deserter, always with an eye out for
time-saving shortcuts, or a reviewer. If the former, well
done. If the latter, hello! Did you know the proceeds from
this book go to restoring the sight of kittens orphaned by
climate change?

What was this book all about? In 'Childhood' (or
somewhere) we mentioned in passing the simple dreamy
delight of staring out of the window; from a train, perhaps, or your front room, or maybe while sitting an
important exam. A little moment of respite from life's
factory, an owl-eyed pause before a blurred, faraway
world.

When did this become a bad thing? From the age of five you're supposed to have better things to do, until you're in your eighties and you're finally allowed to get back to it without some state-sponsored do-gooder or bland corporate overachiever snapping you out of your reverie with a difficult question, the threat of detention or, worse, small talk.

Where do these people think ideas come from? Or solutions, revelations, peace, *humanity*? We think they know damn well where they come from. And that's why we're allowed no downtime, no time to reflect or cogitate, no moments of introspection – lest more people reach the same conclusion as us: *we were made to muck about.*

Get happy

'You wasted your time dreaming/dozing/playing/chatting/down the pub . . .' Hang on a minute. That's not wasting time, that's the *best time*. It's the time that makes us happy. It's what we should aspire to.

As a species, evolution will take care of us, one way or another (probably the other). And on a personal level, what does a life of doing things we don't much care for matter if we are not happy? What does it matter if we are materially rich but imaginatively caged and creatively poor? If we are loaded but miserable? It is our contention that if we are not happy, we are doing something wrong; it is our intention that, by eliminating the causes of unhappiness, we get happy.

Early research (which we would be pleased to continue on receipt of further funding) suggests that we worry too much, don't relax enough and could laugh a good deal more. Not wry smiles or tiny titters, but fits of giggles, barrelling guffaws and pig-snorting, floor-rolling belly laughs. As mentioned previously, if you can find people who can do that to you, never let them go. You could be laughing more of the time.

Of course, one man's recipe for happiness may not apply to everyone. Perhaps some are happy devoting themselves to the interests of others, pursuing a career, amassing a fortune or continually moaning. We appreci-ate we are all different (some of us) and it is for this reason that we do not force our philosophy upon others, nor prey on the needy or the gullible. We simply say no to sterility, no to uniformity and are compelled to leave our insights, born of lives lived full, in the form of this book, that can be passed from generation to generation, so that some may know that they are not alone, that there exist people like them, the Deserters.

Also, it beats working.

Celebrate good times, come on

If there's one thing that we have learned while travelling the globe in search of enlightenment and the best '2 for 1' offers, it is this: it's never too late to celebrate. Nor too early.

'Don't count your chickens before they're hatched,' goes the popular but erroneous idiom. Why not? If you celebrate having three chickens, only to find you've got one, at least you've been out and had a ruddy lovely time. Plus you've got chicken for dinner.

The Dulwich Raider insists on opening a bottle of the finest discounted wine at the merest hint of good news. By the time he's had his good fortune confirmed, he's already celebrated it nine times. If the expected windfall doesn't happen, he will have traded the stress of waiting and hoping for a fruity little Minervois and the clink of glasses with like-minded muckers.

Cheers!

TEST YOUR KNOWLEDGE

1. You arrive at the station to find there are eleven minutes until your train. Do you:

   A) Use the opportunity to pace the platform and jot down some notes for tomorrow's meeting
   B) Pop into the Railway for a swift half
   C) Order a pint, a jug of mulled wine and a bowl of pork scratchings and take the armchair by the fire

2. You receive an email that tomorrow's meeting has been moved to 8 a.m. Do you:

   A) Blow out the gang and tell them you have to get an early night
   B) Congratulate yourself that you primed your Out of Office auto-respond with the message, 'If the meeting is moved any earlier, I might have a doctor's appointment.'

C) Say, 'What email?' aloud to yourself to see how it sounds

3. You get a text from your boss asking if you're 'running late' for the meeting. Do you:

A) Take a cab to work, obliterating your morning's earnings

B) Reply, 'Train delayed while I give CPR to fellow passenger. Start without me and make sure Simon takes proper minutes this time'

C) Reply, 'I am not running late, I am eating a fried egg sandwich'

4. You accidentally leave the house without your phone. Do you:

A) Get your other half to Uber it to you at work

B) Spend the morning on Facebook, LinkedIn and Twitter letting everyone know you are without your phone

C) Lie in the park after lunch and consider cancelling your contract with O2

5. You are asked to pick up some vegetables for dinner on your way home. Do you:

A) Buy aubergine to be sliced, baked and eaten with a fresh plum tomato salsa and extra virgin olive oil

B) Pick up a tin of boiled potatoes, because with a tin of boiled potatoes and some vegetable oil you are only ever minutes away from something resembling chips
C) Buy chips

6. A perfect storm of children's parties, double cookery class and a cancelled dental appointment leaves you with a free afternoon. Do you:

A) Finally get round to those shelves – they won't put themselves up
B) Retrieve the chocolate you hid in the salad crisper and spend the day on the sofa
C) Pint, pint, doobie, pint; game, pint, curry

7. Your neighbour abandons a sofa at the end of your street. Do you:

A) Tut loudly and alert the council
B) Realise it's much nicer than yours and drag it into your yard
C) Install a fridge and some speakers, call up some mates and throw an impromptu al fresco street sofa party

8. A friend texts to say she's bringing US movie star Leonardo DiCaprio along to your weekly catch-up. Do you:

A) Fit in a quick shower and a visit to the hairdresser to look your best for the selfies

B) Make do with a 'French bath' in the lavs and a spray of toilet freshener

C) Text back, 'When, oh when, will they leave us alone?'

9. An alarming encounter with a mirror convinces you that you need to lose some weight. Do you:

A) Give up alcohol immediately and sign up with a gym

B) Get some friends involved in some creaky sports so that at least you can go to the pub afterwards

C) Contract an unsightly viral disease and lose a week – and 10 lbs – shivering in your lovely bed

10. With Christmas approaching your heart sinks at the prospect of buying presents for the extended family. Do you:

A) Spend days splashing out on overpriced tat that no one will ever use

B) Buy a dozen copies of this very book and distribute them among delighted relatives

C) Inform the family that this year you will be making a small donation on their behalf to your local off-licence

Mostly As

Christ. In a sense, we can only admire you. You plainly have not taken the slightest bit of notice of anything we have said. You *could* try starting the book again but really, you might be better off giving it to a friend, if you have any.

For the time wasted in crafting this book for you we ask that you compensate us with immediate effect.*

Mostly Bs

Well done. You exhibit a robust understanding of the principles of shirking, slacking and messing about. At times, you may be able to go a step further, to push your personal boundaries, but there is no point running until you can walk, or indeed walking until you've had a nice sit-down and a cup of Deserter tea, available now at a discounted price.*

Mostly Cs

Congratulations, you have been selected to become an advisory professor on our prospective Deserter online 'sofa learning' course and to receive full certification therein, thereon and thereabouts.*

Once certified, you are permitted to use the title 'Professor of Deserterism' on all correspondence, to attend

---

* Please send a cheque for £199 to the publisher

wet-led educational board meetings whenever you need something convenient to put in your calendar and to have Des, the running man symbol, tattooed on the inside of your lower lip.

Refund Form

I hereby certify that I want my money back, you charlatans.

Name: _____

Address: _____

Email address: _____

Bank: _____

Credit or debit card number: _____

Card security code (CSC) *What is this?*: _____

PIN: _____

Mother's maiden name: _____

First pet: _____

Favourite teacher: _____

Passwords: _____

(Please fill out *all* sections)

Tell us why you would like your money back (please only tick one at a time):

- *Littered with dangerous inaccuracies and made up 'facts'* ☐
- *Too much fucking swearing* ☐
- *Not enough fucking swearing* ☐
- *Too many drug references* ☐
- *Too little drug references* ☐
- *Poor grammar* ☐
- *It changed my life and now I'm skint* ☐

Send this form to the publisher

---

* Not sure

ACKNOWLEDGEMENTS

Rima, Anna, Club, Nationalise Fun, Southey Brewing, Helena, Tom Witcomb, Unbound, Richard Jeffrey, Dom Eames, Dan Jestico, Andy Taylor, Emily Medley, Antony Medley (whose name we misspelt in the last book, for which apollogies), Richard Collins, Miranda Ward, Zelda Rhiando and, of course, Malcolm Bennett. And a massive thank you to everyone who supported the book, pre-publication. In a way, this is all your fault.

Unbound is the world's first crowdfunding publisher, established in 2011.

We believe that wonderful things can happen when you clear a path for people who share a passion. That's why we've built a platform that brings together readers and authors to crowdfund books they believe in – and give fresh ideas that don't fit the traditional mould the chance they deserve.

This book is in your hands because readers made it possible. Everyone who pledged their support is listed below. Join them by visiting unbound.com and supporting a book today.

Karen Bartlett

Perry Bartlett

Michael Bate

Peter Beagley

Lucy Bealing

Betsy Bearden

Harriet Beaumont

Mike Beavan

Iain Bell

Michaela Benkova

Paul Bentley

Steve Berry

Tim Bird

Jo Blackwell

David Blagbrough

Mark Blakeway

Noel Blanden

James Blewett

Joanna Boffey

Caroline Bourne

Rachel Bowyer

Longfield Branch

Stuart Brett

Jon Brice

Tim Brice

Karen Briggs

Andrew Brooks

Sean Brosnan

Louise Brown

David Bryan

Frances Buckley

Simon Bucknall

Masis Bugoz

Tim Burrows

Richard Burton

David Cameron

Neil Campbell

Peter Campbell

Xander Cansell

David Cantrell

Darryl Chamberlain

Hamish Champ

Samantha Chaperon

Andy Charalambous

Nick Christian

Anji Clarke

Christopher Clawson

Ralph Clayton

Nikki Coates

Paul Coombs

Jean Coulson

Joe Cox

Alex Crane

Alison Cresswell

Mark Crilley

Mike Crilly

Dan Crimes

Matthew Cross

Keith Crowhurst

Mary Cusack

CWE

Rob Dagley

John Dallimore

Michael Davies

Tracy Davis

Jake Dawson

Anthony Denny

Rebecca Denton

Daniel Derrett

Stephen Desmond

Rob Dickinson

Phil Douglas

Nick Douse

James Dowdeswell

Brenda Downes

Dukes

Mark Dyson

Dominic Eames

Miles Eames

Matt Eastley

Peter Edmondson

Holly Edwards

Steve Edwards

Phoebe Egg McCluskey

Max Ellis

Peter Faiers

Mike Fairbrass

John Fairlamb

Ian Faragher

Jenty Farr

Sam Faulkner

Lucy Ferguson

Sarah Finigan

Jan Fjeld

Em Fleming

Steven Foreman

Matt Foulds

Richard Fradgley

Lovell Fuller

Josh Gaillemin

Neil Gardner

Garth Garland

Guy Garside

Nicola Gatt

Paul Gill

Diane Glynn

Ian Gordon

Keith Graham

Catherina Gray

Lucy Grimshaw

Henri Grumbridge

Simon Gunning

Cris Hale

Joe Hall

Paul Hamilton

Nick Hanks

Stephen Hardingham

Andrea Harman

Becky Harrington

Tim Harris

Duncan Hart

Keith Hatch

Brixton Hatter

heideewickes

Mark Helm

Susan Hickey

Martin Hills

Ben Hockman

Simon Hogg

Mark Holmes

Matt Hooper

Chris Hornby

Dan Houghton

Mark Howarth

Bec Hu

Peter Hudak

Andy Huggett

Ayo Hughes

Melanie Hughes

Stephen Hunnisett

Steve Hutchings

Chris Jackson

Niall Jackson

Harvey James

Byron Jaye

Matt Jelliman

Jay Jernigan

Dan Jestico

Stephen Jewkes

Darren Johnston

Emmy Maddy Johnston

Fraser Jopp

Guy Joseph

Eoin Keating

Clare Keeble

Geoff Keen

Supporters

Sean Kemplay

Brad Kenyon

Hugh Keogh

Dan Kieran

James Kinnersly

Toby Kirby

Karen Klomp

Michael Lachmann

Shaun Laird

Benjamin Lawson

Chris Le Corney

John Le Corney

Jonathan Leake

Barry Lee

Isobel Lees

Adrian Lightly

Bernadette Lintunen

Tim Livesey

Chris Lockie

Chris Lofts

Clare Loops

James Lush

Anna Lyaruu

Cheryl Lygo

Bryan Lynch

Josh Lyons

Ollie Lyons

Pete Lyons

Emily Magee

Peter Maguire

Peter Manners

Anthony Maplesden

Chris Marchington

Robert Marsh

Albert Marshall

Andy Martin

Ian Martin

Lisa Martinez

Ross Masters

David Matkins

James Mayne

Stephen McCarthy

Phoebe McCluskey

Lesley McFadyen

Alec McGill

Andy McGrath

Andrew McIntosh

Mike McKenna

KJ McLean

Ben McNamee

Roddy McVicar

Laurence Meehan

Keith Meyer
Roger Miles
Bob Millar
Will Miller
Trevor Mitchell
John Mitchinson
Amy Moore
Andrew Moore
Allan Morley
Arita Morris
Nicola Morris
Stephen Morris
Steve Morris
Kate Mulley
Carlo Navato
Stanislav Nikolov
Chris North
Laurence O'Toole
Maryann O'Connor
Brendan O'Duffy
Phil Oakes
Derek Oakley
Kevin Offer
Gemma Oliver
Onion
Peter Orr

Duncan Palmer
Simon Palmer
Gavin Parker
Tristan Parker
John Parkhouse
David Parnell
Isaac Parnell
Andrew Parsons
Charlotte Pearce Cornish
Jon Perry
Anji Petersen
Andrew Phillips
Justin Pollard
Steve Pont
Andrew Potapa
James Powell
Russell Prebble
Mr. Proktor
Sareta Puri
Chloe Raison
Claire Raison
Jack Raison
Vincent Raison
Vijay Raman
Shannon Randall
Amanda Ranford

Supporters

Ean Ravenscroft
Jonny Rawlings
Rob Richardson
Geoff Rideout
Colin Ridgway
Andrea Rieger
Con Riordan
Common Rioters
Edward Robbins
Steve Ronksley
Paul and Harriet Ruffley
Stevie Russell
Zoe Sadler
Christoph Sander
Sarah and Andy G
Tom Sargeant
Carol Sayles
Tim Scott
Andrew Seaman
Martin Searle
Mike Shaw
Lloyd Shepherd
Matt Sheppard
Michael Sheppard
Phil Sherburn
Thomas Sherriff

Ollie Ship
Ben Sibley
Simba & Nin
@Sir_Stefan
David Skeates
Skirky Skirky
Matboy Slim
Fred Smith
Howard Smith
Laurence Smith
Matthew Smith
Richard Soundy
John Spowage
Lianne Starns
Martin Stevens
Gary Stewart
Jan Stöver
Peter Streets
Andrew Sturtevant
Gill Sutherland
Martin Taylor
Neil Taylor
Simon Taylor
Andy Telemacque
Pudsy The Barber
Dafydd Thomas

Tim Thomas @
  timofnewbury
Nicholas Thompson
David Thomson
Matt Thomson
David Tickle
Greg Tinker
Graham Tomlinson
TonyMo
Bert Trautmann
Alistair Twiname
Jessica Tyler
Akane Vallery Uchida
Adaesi Ukairo
Jim Urpeth
Gerrard Veerman
Chris Walton
Sam Warburton
Thomas Ward
Vicky Warner
Campbell, Caroline &
  James Watson

David Watts
Chris Webb
Jake Wetherall
Jason Whitaker
Kirsty White
Leanne White
Charlotte Whitfield
Heide Wickes
Emily Wighton
Robert Willeke
Nick Williams
Tom Williams
Richard Wiseman
Jan Wisz
Pete Worth
Ed Wray
Matt Wright
Ellie Wythe
Warren Yates